For the Love of HER Life

Summer Edition

Compiled by Kit Hinkle and Elizabeth Dyer with the
Writing Team at A Widow's Might/aNew Season

ISBN:1499676255
ISBN-13:9781499676259

DEDICATION

You know the walk of solitude after losing your husband. You long for comfort from those who know your ache and can offer the kind of Hope and encouragement that can only come from the Lord through voices of those who have been there.

May you be blessed with our voices as you climb out from this difficult season. May you bless another when she walks in aNew Season, needing comfort during the early stages of loss.

Job 29:13b

Making the widow's heart sing for joy

Preface:

We've talked about placing a devotional book in the hands of widows since the start of A Widow's Might in 2009 and well into the birth of our umbrella ministry, aNew Season. Finally--here it is. When I think of all the ladies not yet online now being able to access these writings, my heart melts.

I picture **For the Love of Her Life**, our book of daily devotions, as a night-table book. One that perhaps someone got for her as a gift of love, knowing how much she is hurting. And at first it sits next to her, unopened.

Until at some point, she's up late at night and needs to hear from other widows. Finally she'll pull it from her night table to begin reading, letting the comfort of Christ wash over her.

These daily devotionals come straight from our website. They have been proven over the years to bring comfort--the kind that lasts beyond the feel-good hug or reassuring smile, because they bring the comfort of God's Truth.

aNew Season Ministries ministers in the trenches of grief and beyond grief into victorious living through a walk with Christ. For the widow, when it seems no one else understands because they haven't lived it, anewseason.net is just a click away and able to minister to her.

We pray that this devotional becomes a way for a widow's friends and family to reach out to her. How many times have I been asked to mentor a widow, speak to her--tell her her life isn't over. How many times have a widow's loved ones begged me to let her know that she has purpose and there are healthy ways to deal with grief?

And I do. And so do all the writers on our team.

But what about the widow who hasn't physically come across our path?

This devotional book can be given to her right there when the loss is fresh. It's like giving her a whole network of many women who have successfully navigated grief--women of many ages and situations with one thing in common--the knowledge that Christ is the answer to healing.

When the funeral is done and everyone's gone home, she will eventually find herself in that place-- face to face with her solitude. That's when her friends and family will want this devotional, written by many, to comfort her. As she reads through story after story, she'll get it. She's not alone. Many have walked before her--joyfully.

We've decided to publish these devotionals in three month seasonal cycles. We have enough for a year-long daily devotional, but to publish it in one book would make for a large book unless we abridged the writers' work or made the font so small it would become hard to read.

We pray you or your loved one will be blessed by these writings and hope to engage with you at our conferences or online at anewseason.net

God bless you!
Kit Hinkle

Prologue:

My prayer is that, as you read these daily devotions, you will be encouraged to live life again. You are a beautiful daughter of the King and He has more left for you to experience and give to others in this life. The writers at A Widow's Might/aNew Season are so blessed with the opportunity to share our writings with you as we journey together on the path of widowhood. Your heart will sing again.

~Elizabeth Dyer~

Introduction:

Summer

To the reader of our devotionals for the months of June, July, and August:

The breeze of summer can brighten our hearts with a light and airy hope. They can also deepen our pain with a caressing reminder of the love we lost. We pray you will settle in with us during your quiet time each day and read how over a dozen women each faced the same loss you have and have endured the summers as you are enduring. Not only endured but grown and drew closer to each other and to our Father in Heaven who loves you.

~Kit Hinkle and Elizabeth Dyer~

June

June 1
Holy Moses! (or Be the Moses in Your Home)
By Elizabeth Dyer

Moses said to the Lord, "Pardon your servant, Lord. I have never been eloquent...I am slow of speech and tongue."... The Lord said to him, "Now go; I will help you speak and will teach you what to say." But Moses said, "Pardon your servant, Lord. Please send someone else."
Exodus 4:10-13 NIV

Moses. He called me Moses!

I miss it, the sound of his voice calling me that silly name.

I am not sure how it even started. Perhaps it began when he spelled Mom. M-O-M became Mo, then Mo became Mosay. Finally he landed with Moses. Yep, it makes no better sense when I write it out here than it did when he would say it out loud!

But how I wish I could hear him say it out loud again! He has been gone only a few months, and I've already forgotten the sound of his voice calling from the other room.

Little did I know how appropriate and perhaps prophetic that name would be.

Moses. I *am* like a little Moses, leading my little band of Israelites (well, actually, children) to the Promised Land.

Moses wasn't very excited about being the leader of the Israelites. He made excuses. "I'm no good at speaking. I wasn't raised like the Israelites." For crying out loud, he had even murdered an Egyptian! "Pardon Your servant", Moses says in those verses. Moses figured God must have forgotten about those tidbits of disqualifying information.

Am I any different? I make excuses to God. I tell him I don't qualify. I can't keep track of money in my checkbook. I can't help with the advanced math homework. "Pardon Your servant," I tell Him, "but I have control and co-dependency issues! Just ask my counselor!" Surely God has forgotten how ill-prepared I am to lead alone. You name an excuse, and I have probably used it at some point or another.

How did God react to Moses' "Pardon Your servant"? He just gave Moses His promise of accompanying him and teaching him. He supplied a godly confidence. God stepped into the story and used the weaknesses of the characters to create a beautiful masterpiece of His design. He reached through the excuses and pardon me's and gave Moses the confidence to lead because He was going along. Like Moses, I also must go before God with my inadequacies.

How does God my Father react to MY excuses? He quietly reminds me that my "competence comes from God" (2 Corinthians 3:5)

I pray for strength when I want to be weak. To lead when all I want to do is follow. To stand when I just want to curl up in a ball.

The whining Israelites wore Moses down and Moses went to God about the Israelites, reminding God that the Israelites belonged to Him.

I do the same. I often remind God that these are HIS children, not mine. When I get to that place, I remember what God promised Moses that "I will help you...I will teach you."

When I didn't think I could be strong one more minute, He gave me strength. When I wanted to stay in bed and just be alone, God sent hugs and kisses from a sweet innocent youngster. When I couldn't stand firm another minute, He held up my arms in the battle.

God keeps intervening just like the cloud-pillar by day and the fire-pillar by night. God sends friends to keep a kid overnight. God sends a godly man to take my son to dinner and a movie. God sends a sister who knows all of my past to take my hand and pull me to breakfast. He says to me, "I will help you...I will teach you."

He knows how we don't qualify, and that is exactly why we do qualify. Totally dependent on God. Every Day. Every Way.

Dear Father, Thank You that there is nothing in me that qualifies me to lead my family. I am weak and fainthearted. Give me eyes to see a special moment this week where You helped me or taught me. Lead me when I am ready to quit. Remind me to depend on Your strength daily and not my own. Allow me time to meditate on all You are blessing me with, and all I can be today. In Jesus' Name, Amen

Sisters who are raising your husband's children... be the Moses in your home!

June 2
Grieving Gracefully
By Teri Cox

Then Job arose, tore his robe, and shaved his head;
and he fell to the ground and worshipped
Job 1:20-22 NKJV

My grief journey over the past seventeen months has taken me to many places, physically, emotionally, and spiritually. Because I am and have been in a place of leadership for several years, it pressed on me from the very beginning of this journey that people were watching.

Would I turn my back on God and let anger settle in my spirit and break my relationship with Him, or would I cling to Him and love Him through the storm which threatened to drown me?

If I'm going to be real--and I am--I would have to tell you there was a time earlier in my life when I was arrogant enough, broken enough, and angry enough at God to turn my back on Him and walk away.

I remember literally shaking my fist at Heaven, telling God I would get back with Him when I could--but it wasn't then. He was God! He knew how mad I was, and that I was done with Him for a while.

I lived my life in self-indulgent behavior which broke the heart of my Savior every day for two long years. Oh, how thankful I am for a God of mercy and second chances! Somewhere in the middle of my finding my way back to God, I found His amazing gift for me: my late husband Daryl.

So now, with only twelve short years of life together and me fully knowing how incredibly blessed I was every single day of that marriage, I again had a choice. What would I do--turn to the world or turn to The Cross?

This time, there was no hesitation, no stutter, no misplaced rage, just me leaning so hard into God all I could do was repeat *"His GRACE is sufficient, HIS grace is sufficient, His grace IS sufficient."*

It was not because I am some "super Christian" I can repeat and believe these words, but because my marriage to a Godly man changed me from the inside out, making my relationship with Christ stronger than it had ever been.

If I turned my back during this storm, to me it was the same as saying my marriage had not meant anything.. that it had not impacted me...grown me... matured me.

So I asked a pastor friend of mine who'd reminded me people were watching, "How do I do this gracefully?"

He said, "I don't know. But I do know that grace has **nothing to do with you** and **everything to do with God**."

Wow, what incredible wisdom.

Grieving gracefully, I'm still trying to figure out exactly what that means, what it looks like, and how to do it. But now, instead of worrying about who is watching, I just know that *El Roi-the God who sees me* is all that matters. In the middle of Hagar's affliction this was her cry.

He sees you, dear sisters, He sees you. He still thinks you are lovely and you are His special girl. So do not let anyone stand in judgment of your grief journey. It is yours and God's to complete. Lean into Him and let Him carry you through. Amen

June 3
Invisible or Hidden?
By Kathleen Beard

For you died, and your life is now hidden with Christ in God
Colossians 3:3 NIV

I will never forget in the early days after John moved to heaven, going to a grocery store and passing another shopper who looked in my direction, our eyes meeting. I suddenly felt surprised that someone could still see me. I was aware of feeling invisible. I thought about that a great deal over the next few days—why did I feel invisible? It occurred to me that because in Christ we were "one flesh," it was as if literally, because we were one flesh, half of "me" was gone and I felt mostly invisible. The experience of suddenly feeling invisible brought home the whole truth about being one flesh with John.

Was I really invisible? Or was it that I was *hidden?* According to Colossians 3:3, we died with Christ and our lives are "hidden with Christ in God." It is not simply that we are going to die someday, but we died in Him and He now lives His resurrected life in us. This is big stuff—really way too big for a widow trying to navigate her way through the early stages of grief, but sometimes it is at that precise time that God brings home to our awareness these big truths. He brought it home to me—when it seemed my fogged mind could not negotiate any thought bigger than how to breathe the next breath.

But that is how it happened—He had something huge to teach me about life and death and in this verse, He was speaking "above-the-line" stuff and it was making sense. He was telling me that my [self] life had died twenty years before as soon as I made Him my Lord and Savior and that the "old" John had died nine years before when he believed in and received Christ. As one flesh, we were both alive in Christ and hidden with Christ in God. Now that he had moved to Heaven, I was feeling invisible, but I was really only experiencing being hidden in Christ. John was now fully alive and no longer hidden at all—he was face to face—one with Christ and finally complete!

I still do sometimes feel like half of that one flesh, but more often now I am living in the truth that my life is hid with Christ in God—in my actuality—not just my theology. I am becoming comfortable being hidden and invisible, as long as I am hidden *with* Christ and *in* God. There is simply no place safer.

Lord My God; my Rock and my strength, how I thank You that You are taking me through these mysterious phases of the grieving process and managing it all for me. I love you so much Abba. Amen

June 4
Take It Back!
By Erika Graham

Then he said to them, "My soul is overwhelmed with sorrow to the point of death. Stay here and keep watch with me." Going a little farther, he fell with his face to the ground and prayed, "My Father, if it is possible, may this cup be taken from me. Yet not as I will, but as you will."

Matthew 26: 38-39 NIV

"I'm sorry Mommy, I wish I could take it back!"

That's what my daughter said through tears, as she was reprimanded for getting frustrated with her sometimes pesky little brother and pushing him head over heels off the bed.

How about you? Like my girl, do you ever wish you could take something back? A harsh word...A sticky situation...A painful time.

For me, there are really far too many "take it backs" to list. But I do have one that stands out the most; the day, almost four years ago, that my husband took his own life. That horrific day, I stood in the funeral home and cried out to God, pleading from depths I didn't know existed. I begged Him to take it back, believing He could do this miracle!

But "take it back" wasn't possible, so I shifted my prayers and my cries rather quickly.

"Please Lord, use this...for Your glory!"

My husband's life wouldn't be defined by one horrible moment, because I serve a God that's so much bigger. Even as my faith was being tested beyond anything I could have fathomed, I believed

God would use it if He chose not to take it back or prevent it.

I've seen Him doing that every single day in both big and small ways. He has been there through the dark times, when I could barely muster up the strength to get out of bed, when my kids cried themselves to sleep, or woke up from a nightmare crying out for their daddy. God healed us and moved us beyond those early dark days. He's provided us with so much help and support.

He has restored us a little more with each passing day. He has brought joy and hope back to our home. God is using our story to bring honor and glory to Him every time He gives me the opportunity to share it.

When I needed it most it brought me great comfort to read in God's word that I am not alone in the "take it back" department; Moses (Exodus 3:11), Jonah (Jonah 1:3), Job (23:4) and even Christ himself all at some point wanted God to "take it back".

Yes even Jesus!!

In the book of Matthew, Jesus is in the Garden of Gethsemane and the full awareness of what lay ahead weighs heavily on Him. He prayed and cried out because Jesus knew full well God could take it; but He also knew if God didn't remove this He was going to use it.

Did He ever… Jesus died on the cross for us all, so through Him we may have eternal life with Him. How awesome!

Sisters, no matter where you are in your grief journey, no matter how you lost your beloved husband, we can trust His will. We can rest assured that in this and all things whether the Lord takes it back or not, He will use it for His glory (Romans 8:28).

What a comforting promise!

Father God, help me to trust You and Your plan for my life. Even though I didn't get to see You "take it back", help me to see and feel the many ways You use my loss and my story to bring glory to You. In Your Matchless Name, Amen

June 5
A Different Perspective: What if My Husband Wasn't All that and More?
By Rene Zonner

Finally, brothers and sisters, whatever is true, whatever is noble, whatever is right, whatever is pure, whatever is lovely, whatever is admirable-if anything is excellent or praiseworthy-think about such things.

Philippians 4:8 NIV

Can I be honest with you? I mean, really honest? Sometimes I read the posts and comments from my widow sisters on the blog, and I just feel out of place.

So many of you had amazing husbands who were Godly men—the spiritual leaders of your home and wonderful fathers.

That wasn't my husband.

John professed a faith in Christ, but he rarely cracked open his Bible and never attended church with us. He was not the spiritual leader I craved. He wasn't a very involved dad either. Often he chose watching a game on TV, going out with friends, or even just taking a nap over spending time on a family activity.

He wasn't a bad person, and he was doing the best he could. His own father walked out on the family when John was a little boy. He grew up with a terrible and abusive step-father. He wasn't taken to church or taught the importance of a faith community. He just didn't have positive male role models in his life to teach him how to be a father and husband.

So when I read about your wonderful husbands, I feel a longing to have the type of memories you do. I find myself wishing we would have had more time for John to grow and change into the man I hoped he would become.

I'm not the only one, right? It feels like it sometimes, though. Surely there are others who had a less than perfect marriage. As widows we can be reluctant to speak of anything less than the good about our late husbands. It just doesn't feel right to say something negative about a man who isn't here to defend himself.

So we keep our mouths shut. We stuff our feelings inside. We retreat from community because we don't feel like anyone can relate to us. But in doing so, we isolate ourselves. Isolation is the enemy's favorite weapon against us.

As we near special days, this feeling of being alone, of being the only one with a less than ideal situation, grows. There is so much talk this time of year about all the wonderful things that Dad does. Widows with children look for ways to celebrate the father their husband was. There are lots of great ideas, but none seem to fit our own situation.

So what do we do?

Are there things you have focused on with your children? Think about this and tomorrow I will give you some ideas I have had. If you had a godly father/husband in your home, thank God right now for that example for your children.

June 6
A Different Perspective Continued
By Rene Zonner

Yesterday I began talking about my situation and the father of my children. I left you with a question. What do we do if we had a less than ideal situation with Father's Day at this time of year?

I have a few ideas.

First know you are not alone. Not every widow is mourning the loss of an amazing husband and father. That doesn't make your grief any less. You may have craved a stronger marriage, a Godly husband but you still miss and mourn the man he was. And, like me, you likely grieve for what could have been. The enemy would have you believe that no one else is feeling the same but you can rest assured that at least this widow is in the same boat with you.

Next, focus on the positive. Philippians 4:8 comes to mind. It states "...whatever is true, whatever is noble, whatever is right, whatever is pure, whatever is lovely, whatever is admirable-if anything is excellent or praiseworthy-think about such things." In our humanness, it is easy to focus on what we would have changed in our husbands. But our whole attitude can change when we choose to focus on what he did right....even if it's only one thing.

My children are still young and we talk about Dad a lot. I want them to have a positive, but realistic image of their father. We talk honestly about the things that we would like to have been different, but we talk even more about the things that were good.

"Sure, Dad didn't do a lot of the fun activities with us, but he worked really hard, and some crazy hours to provide for us."

"No, Dad didn't go to church with us but he never complained about our decision to go, even when it meant not spending time with him."

We are honest and realistic about who he was, but still honor the good, the lovely and the praiseworthy.

And my last piece of advice is to be honest with others about the shortcomings in your marriage and your husband. Pretending things were different doesn't help. Avoiding the community of other widows hurts your healing journey. I have found that since I took the steps to be more open about the shortcoming of my late husband, other widows have been more open about sharing things that could have been better in their marriages. They share how the men they thought were perfect husbands and fathers also had areas of weakness. As others talked honestly, I felt less alone.

So, as we near the day for celebrating the men in our lives, let's be honest about the men our husbands were…both for the good and the not so good.

Heavenly Father, I pray as I approach a day all about celebrating someone who is no longer with me. It can be such a hard day for so many reasons. I pray You will bring good memories to mind. I ask that You allow me to focus on the good, right and noble in our late husbands. But I also ask that You help me to be honest about the shortcomings. Thank You for giving me the chance to draw comfort and peace from others in similar situations. Amen

June 7
A Happy Father's Day?
By Liz Anne Wright

Praise be to the God and Father of our Lord Jesus Christ, the Father of compassion and the God of all comfort, who comforts us in all our troubles, so that we can comfort those in any trouble with the comfort we ourselves receive from God.
2 Corinthians 1:3-4 NIV

Father's Day. Any way you slice it, this can be a tough holiday as a widow…especially a widow with children. The fewer years you are into this journey, the harder this day seems to be.

Dear sisters, you are not alone! Just like you, those of us on the writing team have to deal with this holiday…and all its implications and ramifications. We on the writing team for A Widow's Might each have our own opinions and traditions…ways to help make it a good or at least a passable day for us.

We would like to share some of our ideas with you. We pray that our own traditions and methods may give ideas on how to deal with your own Father's Day. We pray that God will be glorified, not only by what we do for Father's Day, but by your Father's Day as well.

So...here, in a slightly different format, we present our ideas. May they bless you!

<u>Kit</u>: I have always believed Father's Day to be particularly important for children who have lost their father--why? Because it's an opportunity for the surviving mother to recall for them the elements of who their daddy was--those particular elements that model Christ for them. Children who grow up without a daddy run the risk of having trouble identifying with a Father God Whom they can trust. We who recognize this and can get our emotions around our own grief under control can minister intentionally to our children. We can help fill in those blanks of what Dad means to them...which leads to what does God mean to them. With boys, I've intentionally turned Father's Day into Brother's Day-- using that day to write to each boy, a letter recalling ways over the past year I've seen them grow and mature into the Christ-like man that Dad was. That not only gives them recognition and something to look forward to, but also reinforces the parts of Dad that model Christ for them.

<u>Linda</u>: The first Father's Day for us came about a month after my husband passed. My daughter

suggested she and I spend some time together - we went and got some frozen yogurt and shared memories about him. The second Father's Day was a bit easier - she decided to spend the day alone using all of his power tools to build a piece of furniture - that gave me such joy - knowing that she had inherited her dad's talent and was using those tools on that particular day! As the initial raw pain of my loss begins to subside, the wonderful memories of specific occurrences are starting to surface. I have been giving some thought to writing those out and presenting them to my daughter at some point - perhaps next Father's Day.

<u>Rene</u>: We have kept Father's Day fairly low key. The first year after John's death, the boys did each make a small gift for their dad that we took out and laid on his headstone. Then we went to lunch somewhere we thought he would have liked.

June 8
More Father's Day Ideas from our Writers:

<u>Nancy</u>: Last year was our first without Mark. We stayed home from church. Seems like everywhere we went, there were huge banners proclaiming sales for dads, cards, etc. It was tough. We hibernated for the day, just being together the three of us. This year, I've asked the boys to think about what they want to do to celebrate. Again, we will refrain from church. I cannot go and watch as dads are honored, while my boys sit

beside me without theirs. I cannot sing "Faith of our Fathers" yet, but hope someday that I will be able to. My younger son wants to get balloons to release to heaven for his dad. I will encourage them to attach notes to them, and we will read them aloud before releasing.

Liz: On this day that honors fathers, we instead choose to focus on what we do have, not what we have lost. And that is truly a lot! Every year since Keith died, my boys have figured out cards for the men at church whom God has convicted to be part of our lives. Last year's card said, "As a father figure, you've nailed it." and we included a nail in the cards. We passed out upwards of eighteen cards, and probably could have used a few more. The boys get really excited, dashing around church looking for each of the men. They welcome them with a big hug and present the cards. They even fight over who gets to give cards to which man. The men are touched and sometimes even get a bit teary.

What new idea can you incorporate into your remembrance of Father's Day this year?

June 9
Father's Day
By Danita Hiles

Father's Day. Without another word, I know you get the emotion of those words. Every commercial, every card rack and every rack of carefully folded shirts ready to give 'to your special dad' screams out a reminder of what we have lost and of the future that looms ahead.

For me, this year seems particularly difficult. Maybe because I have daughters; a teenager and preteen struggling to find their place in life.

Recently the fear that I feel for their future is almost paralyzing. I don't feel it for myself as much, but for them.

Fear that the gaping hole left by the loss of their dad will never be filled.

Fear that they will turn to others to fill the space meant for God.

Fear that the lies of the enemy will drown out the truth of God's plan for them. I see choices currently being made because of the empty, and I agonize over the far reaching consequences of those choices.

And yes, I know this fear is not from Him.

I know He tells us over and over to fear not, though I know this, we are still very much in the middle of our journey – not at a place where I can look back with satisfaction and say, 'Wow, in spite of all that, look at the amazing faith God has built in my girls'.

So when you can't explain the 'why?' of the past, and you are fighting fear over the 'what' of the future, all that is left is the right now. Thankfully, in all of the uncertainty, we have the concrete promises found in His word.

Right now here is what I know:

- I know whom I have believed, and am convinced that He is able to guard what I have entrusted to him for that day. 2 Tim. 1:12
- For I know the plans I have for you," declares the LORD, "plans to prosper you and not to harm you, plans to give you hope and a future. Jer. 29:11
- A father to the fatherless, a defender of widows is God in his holy dwelling Psalm 68:5
- But the Lord is faithful, and he will strengthen and protect you from the evil one. 2 Thess. 3:3

The bottom line is this: we have the creator of the universe as our heavenly Father, rejoicing over our kids with singing, directing their paths, providing His guidance and protection.

Happy Father's Day, Lord! I pray You surround me with Your presence as I walk through this Father's Day. May I see You not only as my heavenly Father, but also as father to my kids. Let them know they are not alone in this journey and that You go before them with every step . Amen

June 10
Father to the Fatherless
By Rene Zonner

> *A Father to the fatherless,*
> *a Defender of widows,*
> *is God in His holy dwelling.*
> *Psalm 68:5 NIV*

I recently looked at pictures of my children that were just a couple of years old and was amazed at how much they have changed.

They are all taller. My oldest son is maturing and turning into a young man right in front of my eyes. My younger son has lost a lot of that round baby face he used to have. My daughter is no longer a toddler.

And my husband is missing it all.

It makes me sad to think that John is never going to know the boys as men or my daughter as a woman. It seems unfair that the kids don't have a father cheering them on at their baseball games or that my little girl doesn't have a daddy to take her to the father/daughter dance.

It's been three years since I lost my husband and, in general, I feel I am doing well. I have worked through a lot of my grief and am happy with where my life is going. But when I think about my kids, that progress slips away quickly.

I find myself despairing that the children don't have a daddy in their life to watch them grow and marvel at how much they are changing. I get angry with God for taking John away from them. I worry about their futures and how not having a father around will affect them.

But when I find myself going down that road, I have to stop and change direction. My children may not have an earthly father any longer but they are not fatherless.

Psalm 68:5 tells me that God is a Father to the fatherless. How could I ever ask for a better father for my children? The Creator of the universe, the Master of all that is, specifically states in His word He will be the father for my kids. Because my children don't have an earthly father, they have a special place in God's heart.

I don't know if I have stressed the significance of this enough to my kids. We talk all the time about how God provides for us. We thank Him for all the ways He cares for us. I admit I haven't really thought to talk to them about how God has singled them out in His word. That needs to change.

I want them to realize just how significant this is. They should be in awe of God seeing them as His special children. When they feel different from other kids because they don't have the physical presence of their dad, I will tell them how God is always with them. When they long to have a dad to cheer them on, I will remind them that God is their biggest supporter. When they feel like something is missing in our little family, we will reflect on how our family is complete as long as God is in the center of it.

In order to be the reminder for my children however, I need to remember I'm not alone in this. Oh, there are many days when it feels like I am. It's hard to be the only one who does all the running around, cooking, cleaning, and disciplining. But God is the one who has the responsibility of determining their futures, of planning their lives. He is the one who knows how it's all going to work out and what needs to happen. That's not my job. I need to let God be their Father, I need to stop trying to be both parents. I need to concentrate on what God has laid at my feet and not worry about what he hasn't.

I trust God to make sure my kids beat the statistics which say they will be dysfunctional because they grew up in a single parent home. My God is bigger than any statistic. He can overcome all circumstances. I don't have to let the dark cloud of worry overtake me. Matthew 6:34 says, "Therefore do not worry about tomorrow, for tomorrow will worry about itself."

My children do have a Dad and he knows more about them than I ever will. He loves them more than I ever could. He not only sees the amazing kids they are now, He sees the men and woman they will become.

I'm pretty sure He jumps for joy when they hit a home run.

Father, thank You for loving my children in a way I just can't. Thank You for being a father to them. Help me to remember I am not in this alone. Remind me when the days are tough and long that You are right there with me. I ask for protection over the hearts and souls of all my children. Father God, I know You can do what society says can't be done. I believe that You can lead us in how to raise healthy, emotionally strong, and godly men and women. I know in Christ all things are possible and I claim that promise for my kids. Father to the fatherless, Defender of the widow…this is who You are to me. Amen

June 11
No More Secrets
By Kit Hinkle

What I tell you in the dark, say in the light, and what you hear whispered, proclaim on the housetops.
Matthew 10:27 ESV

I've had a secret.

And God told me to stop whispering it, and instead shout it from the housetops, because all of you who are suffering as I suffered in the first few years of my widowhood need to get in on this secret.

I didn't mean to keep this secret. So often in the spirit of showing compassion for the pain you are in, because I've been there, I've contained my excitement over it.

Here it is…this Christ stuff—in this walk as a widow—it really works! He has really pulled me out of my grief and gave me new life! I can tell you for certain that the healing is real because He has carried me through walking away from a possible new marriage back into a life as a single woman, forgiving strained friendships, and ministering to all of my husband's children as they suffer the loss.

There is a temptation for all of us as widows to stay in the place of missing our husbands. There is a period of time, early in your loss, where remembering him and mourning him without expressing much joy is appropriate, and, for that reason, I've been careful not to upset anyone with being overly upbeat with the truth—that God has accomplished huge healing of the wounds of my widowhood.

I'm realizing I had it backwards. I no longer want to keep my testimony so secret for fear of scaring away readers who don't want to leave that place of longing for their husbands. So please accept my apology up front if that's you, and know I get that—in those first years I clung to the memory of my husband as I should have--it's part of the process.

But here's what I've considered. If I can help you see the healing that has taken place in me over the last five years, you would understand, without a doubt, that Christ is incredible, and He guarantees that you won't need to be lonely forever, simply because you've been widowed! I know that in those first years as I mourned over Tom, I longed to hear stories of women who had gone through that lonely tunnel of widowhood and come out into the light of new life. But somehow, I couldn't find them. So many mentors were relating to my loss without showing me victory over my loss. How I wished someone would shout the truth of God's healing from the housetops as Jesus so beautifully put it in Matthew 10:27.

So I will continue my writing and testimony of healing to you, now with much rejoicing, because I want someone out there who is hurting to know that you don't need to think of yourself for the rest of your life as living in grief.

God will heal, and you too can then shout from the rooftops how Christ has redeemed you— not just for eternity, but so that you can experience His abundant life here on earth!

I will never forget my husband and his impact on this world. But I will honor him by taking the baton and furthering God's work in his stead, starting by ministering to His widows, one at a time!

June 12
God Is Bigger
By Liz Anne Wright

God. Is. Bigger.

Recently, I put this status on my personal Facebook page. I got quite a few responses, primarily "likes."

As humans, we like to think that God is bigger. We like to have the Big Guy in our corner.

But do we really live like that?

Today, I challenge you, ladies, to *live* like God is bigger:

- bigger than the hole in your heart
- bigger than the money stresses you are facing
- bigger than raising your kids alone
- bigger than being the only single adult in the room
- bigger than special dates on the calendar
- bigger than any aspect of your grief, as complicated and all-encompassing as it is

We have the *God of the Universe* in our corner. Nothing that has happened is a surprise to Him, not even our husbands' passings. He knew what that day would look like before it ever started.

And He holds us in His hands.

Cling to Him, sisters! He is truly all we need. Amen and amen!

June 13
A New Season?
By Kathleen Beard

There is a time for everything,
and a season for every activity under the heavens:
Ecclesiastes 3:1 NIV

When my husband was sick with dementia, I remember how often I would cry out to God— "What is going on? For the past ten years You have sent me out with Your message, teaching and ministering to hurting women. Now all I can do is sit here, watching my husband leave me one brain cell at a time, and I see no light at the end of this tunnel."

Some of the most important words I heard were words which encouraged me that there would be life after this awful thing that had invaded my husband— I needed to know that. I needed to know that He would redeem something out of all of this; something which would bring Him glory because it seemed awfully dim at that point.

Of course, I have written much about the harvest after this time of sitting still, and He did redeem it. John is with Him now, looking right at His face, bowing before Him, singing praise to Him. If that was the only thing that He redeemed, it would be enough. As the Jewish people sing at Passover, "Dayanu" –It would have been enough! But He redeemed so much more and turned that time of deep soul grief into a glorious praise, as He wove my pain into a hymn of praise that now is able to be used as a balm of comfort and healing in the lives of others who face this disease.

I have often pondered the new season that Jesus brought out of that time of grief and pain, and I marvel at how He has woven strands of hope into the fabric of my life as a widow. But it is not the end of my story. While there have been seasons of absolute productive harvests, there have also been new seasons of wells of deep pain as He has allowed other "seasons" into my life that I felt would consume me.

You see, life is not a linear thing—with point A leading to point B, as we often see it on a timeline. Life is made up of seasons, with periods of waiting—hearing nothing from Him, periods of intense emotional pain longing for a break and a drink of cool water, and thankfully, periods of intense moments of His presence—inexpressible joy. If we can but see everything that comes our way as a season, and remember how often the Word of God uses this simple phrase, "And it came to pass…"
It *came ~ to pass.*

God has brought a new season once again into my life, a season of caring for my Mom. My Mom submitted to the Lord, as she has always done, and relinquished her right to drive. My new season now seems to be directed towards a time of sitting still, relinquishing so much of the ministry to the "many" that I have loved, in order to minister to "one." One sweet, humble saint who has given her entire life to ministry to others and now is waiting to see the God whom she has loved and served all these years, face to face. And He is asking me to sit with her, abide in Him with her, give back to her comfort and love for all the years she has given me of comfort and love.

A new season—one that is going to end in sorrow for me, but glory for her, and after I have grieved awhile, He will lead me into the next thing. Always, the next thing.

June 14
His Plan – A New Life!
By Karen Emberlin

> *For I know the plans I have for you, says the Lord.*
> *They are plans for good and not for evil,*
> *to give you a future and a hope.*
> *In those days when you pray, I will listen.*
> *You will find me when you seek me,*
> *if you look for me in earnest.*
>
> *Jeremiah 29:11-13 TLB*

For I know the plans I have for you.....

My husband and I talked a lot about our future and our plans, and yes, we daily sought God's will for our future. The economy had taken a toll on our small business and we did not know exactly what the future held, but we were looking forward to "growing old" together – no matter what God had in store for us!

God had a plan that I had never even thought about for one minute – His plan was to suddenly take my husband "home" and leave me here, alone!! I could not understand how this could be for my good and certainly did not see a future and a hope.

Within three weeks of my husband's death, I had sorted, sold, given away, and finally packed a small amount of our earthly possessions in preparation to move. As I sorted, I tried to keep things that were special to me and represented the forty-eight years we had together. Some dear friends from our church helped with this process and to this day I do not know what happened to a lot of "our stuff".

After the funeral service, my daughter took the fresh flowers from the spray on my husband's casket and hung them upside down in the garage. One of the last things I did before leaving our home was to take the then dried flowers and place them in a plastic box. The box traveled with me from Tennessee to Florida and back to Indiana over a period of fourteen months and has now been in the garage for another year. Even with all of the travel and storage the dried flowers survived! I did not want to give them up, but was not sure what to do with them.

Two weeks ago, my friend and I happened into a small gift shop by mistake. As I was browsing, a small glass box took my eye and I immediately thought about the dried flowers. It didn't take long to purchase it and begin to think about how I could display them.

This glass box has special meaning for me, beginning with the original live flowers that were placed on my husband's casket two years ago representing his life and the love I had for him. Even though the flowers have died (as my husband), to me, the butterfly represents new life or transformation. It has been said that "what the caterpillar calls the end of the world, the Master calls a butterfly". My husband's life on this earth is over, but he is experiencing "new life" in heaven with our Savior! The butterfly is also a reminder to me of the new beginnings in my life as I progress in this new season. And of course I could not leave out my favorite color, purple (amethyst). There are many definitions associated with the purple or amethyst stone such as, royalty, peace, power, protection, wisdom and healing, however, the one definition that speaks to me says amethyst is closely linked to faith. The purple butterfly, the purple flowers, and even my purple insulin pump are daily reminders to me of the faith I have in my Lord and Savior who walks this journey with me every day!

Yes, God's plan was to take my husband home - I know He has a plan for me and tells me "you will find me when you seek me, if you look for me in earnest". Seeking does not always bring a "quick" fix but it causes me to realize I am part of a bigger story. One in which God resolves our disappointments in a way that exceeds our short sight. I have the glorious hope of not only seeing my Savior one day soon, but also seeing my beloved husband again!!

Thank you Lord, for the plans You have for me and each of my dear Sisters. Help me to continue to seek You and press on toward the goal to win the prize for which God has called me heavenward in Christ Jesus. Amen

June 15
Keep Good Faith, Share Good Will
By Nancy Howell

And not only that, but we also glory in tribulations, knowing that tribulation produces perseverance; and perseverance, character; and character, hope.

Romans 5:3-4 NKJV

If there is glory in tribulation, sisters, we have it in each of our homes with a capital "G." For over two years, I have personally experienced tribulations as a sudden widow-single mom to two sons. I have been thrust into situations I had no clue how to handle. I have been forced to become the head of the household, overseeing everything from our finances to home maintenance to parenting decisions to car repair and upkeep, all while my on-going pre-widow responsibilities still hover in the background. How about you?

I jokingly told my sons last night, "I need a wife!"

God made both man and woman to complement each other, bring out the best in one another. Together, they can be a great team. In my marriage, I was extremely lucky. We were a finely-tuned, well-oiled machine that could handle most any problem or situation which presented itself. The oil that kept that machine running? God.

Whenever Mark died, I had to come up with new ways to deal with all the "stuff" continuing to come my family's way. God's word tells us to *glory* (praise, worship, adore, honor, pay homage) *in our tribulations*.

Sometimes glorying in tribulations put in our pathway means simply dealing with them. Putting one foot in front of the other, whenever the grief and pain of our losses threaten to take our breath away, is all we can muster at the time.

Thankfully, the gift of hindsight allows us to look back at that difficult path. From that vantage point, armed with a bit of rest, some healing, and fresh perspective, we find there truly was a bit of glory in the tribulations, the sorrow, the profound grief in those awfully sad circumstances.

The path of a widow is full of adjustments, trials, new experiences, painful memories, and loss. Whenever we give ourselves permission to experience these integral but painful parts of our lives, the end result can be beautiful, just as the scripture reads above.

The apostle Paul knew firsthand about tribulations. He spoke and wrote from countless personal experiences. He knew that *pain and trials and sadness and grief,* when experienced while holding the hand of God, can *produce perseverance.*

What is perseverance? Here's my favorite definition: "*Perseverance* is not giving up. It is persistence and tenacity, the effort required to do something and keep doing it until the end, even if it's hard." For widows, for families struggling to put the pieces of their lives back together after a loss of a husband and father, it means pushing forward. Even when it seems impossible to do.

For my family, it was maintaining a sense of normalcy, in the midst of a hurricane that threatened to consume us after my husband's death. Looking back, I don't know how we did it. But we did "it" over and over and over again, until we began to feel we would survive this.

I knew that more than anything in this world, my husband would want us to live life, to continue having fun. So, we persevered.

Tomorrow I will share more of this keeping of the good faith that we have done.

June 16
Keep Good Faith, Part 2
By Nancy Howell

I started telling you yesterday about the tribulations that came my way after my husband died. And we persevered and survived.

From perseverance, according to Paul, *comes character*.

"Character isn't who you are when life goes your way. Character is who you really are when the bottom falls out." - LeCrae Moore

When the bottom falls out, who are you?

My two boys, now ages eleven and ten, have developed great character since the bottom fell out of their lives. They were great little boys before they lost their daddy, but the level and depth of faith and wisdom they now possess blows this mama away. And I owe it all to the work of our awesome God and Father.

While having a sad moment a couple of nights ago, I hugged my 5'2" ten year old. A tear dropped down my cheek. He smiled, hugged me back, and exclaimed, "Mom, you are a great mom and I love you." I replied, "Ben, do you really think I'm a good mom?" "Yes, Mom, I do. Remember, all you have to do is believe in yourself. That's what I do. Keep good faith and share good will....it's the Golden Rule." As our discussion traversed into areas of faith most young boys don't even think about, I shared with him the official definition of the Golden Rule. But you know, the more I think about it, the more his interpretation makes sense. Yes, indeed, my children are teaching me.

From character comes hope.

Hope? Biblically speaking, hope is "confident expectation." It's a firm assurance that life has meaning. Christians have hope. We know who's going to win in the end. This human life can have grief, tribulations, sickness, death, and numerous other trials. It's just a dress rehearsal for our souls this side of heaven.

Tribulations. Glory. Perseverance. Hope.

Keep good faith, sisters. Share good will. Persevere. Glory in your tribulations. Most of all, never forget that you have hope.

God our Father, I am trying to make sense of the tribulations in my life. I am walking through dark valleys, or climbing over big rocks, or scaling mountains. I am weary. Help me to persevere. Give me strength, wisdom, and peace. The bottom has fallen out of my life, and I seem to have lost sure footing--use these painful experiences as opportunity for growth, for my true character to be revealed. Above all else, let me never abandon hope. Hope of tomorrow, hope of healing, and hope for happiness this side of heaven. In Your sweet son Jesus' name we ask it all, Amen.

June 17
Sovereign
By Sarah Rodriguez

> *The Lord has established His throne in the heavens;*
> *And His sovereignty rules over all.*
> *Psalm 103:19 NASB*

As a new widow I have had some moments recently where I'm really "going there" with The Lord. I've been asking Him some hard questions and even expressing to Him my anger for why things happened in my life the way they did (He knows my thoughts, I may as well voice them). I know none of these thoughts, feelings, or questions are ones that will be rectified any time soon. It has become a part of my process that I will just have to walk through.

I will say through all of my questioning I had one realization that became a breakthrough for me recently. My husband belongs to God. He was my husband second but he was Gods child first. While I will say I loved him more than anyone, there's one person who loved him more, and that is God. My husband Joel was my partner but not my possession. On paper he was committed and "belonged" to me but he didn't really belong to me, he belonged to God. In knowing God I can trust He had my husband in the palm of His hand the whole time and I have to believe He still does. While my hope, prayer and deepest desire was to have my husband with me, I have realized he was God's child first and foremost and God sees and knows more than I ever could. While His viewpoint certainly doesn't make much sense from my vantage point, I can rest in God's love for my husband. I know how deeply I loved Joel, the deepest deep, but God loved him more. I never gave up my life for my husband, Jesus did. When I find myself questioning "why why why" it helps to keep that in perspective. Even though it's not what I want to hear or it still doesn't seem fair, it's still truth.

The Bible talks a lot about God being sovereign. I looked up what that means. It's supreme; preeminent; indisputable. God and Who He is, His power and His authority is indisputable. I argue with God on this situation though. I tell Him day after day I think the right decision would've been for Joel to still be here with us. Still God is sovereign. What's left of my life seems to be in shambles and doesn't make a lick of sense. Still God is sovereign. Joel's life was cut way too short as was my life with him. Still God is sovereign. What lies ahead is unknown and what's behind us is heartbreaking. Still God is sovereign.

This is why I frequently say I say I don't understand, but I trust. It doesn't mean I don't question and it doesn't mean I'm not angry many days. I just know how much I loved Joel and I know Jesus loved him more. If I can't trust the creator of the universe on this, the one who knit together Joel in the womb, who can I trust? At some point, despite every question (and I will keep asking them) my truth has to land on who He is. I know that one day every question will be answered from the one who knows and loves both of us with an unparalleled love. While that doesn't keep me from hurting now it does give me a place to land. And that is safely in the arms of a sovereign God.

June 18
Forgotten?
By Linda Lint

I will not forget you.
Isaiah 49:15 Amplified

There was no paper handy and I really needed to remember that phone number – so, I grabbed the handiest writing instrument and wrote it on the palm of my hand. Well, the instrument that I grabbed happened to be a black permanent marker; and traces of that phone number were visible for several days! That number was not likely to be forgotten!

There's a word that comes to our minds frequently doesn't it –" forgotten"? After the phone calls and the cards stop coming, we begin to feel forgotten. And as time goes on, there are days we wonder if God has forgotten us as well. These are normal feelings, and I will admit to experiencing them at times. It is difficult to feel loved and "remembered" when the one person who always reinforced our existence is no longer with us. No matter what was going on in our lives, we always knew there was that one "special" person who loved us and always "remembered" us. I miss that, and I know you do as well.

But, dear sisters, are we really forgotten? There is **ONE** who thinks of us constantly! This is what He says to us in Isaiah 49:15-16: I will not forget you! Behold, I have indelibly imprinted (tattooed a picture of) YOU on the palm of each of My hands. (Amplified)

After much scrubbing for two or three days, that black permanent marker eventually faded from my hand. But God says He has permanently imprinted a picture of us on the palm of His hands – there forever, indelible - a picture of you – and me. He is telling us He has a picture of us before Him at all times – it can't be scrubbed away. No grief, fear, loneliness, or anxiety can remove our picture from His hands! We are ever before Him.

Yes, He knows our loneliness, and how difficult these times are. And so many, many years ago through His prophet Isaiah He gave us an incredible picture of how He remembers us daily. It is a message of love and comfort sent to hurting hearts like yours and mine, as we travel through these days. Truly it is a message of His love and care.

I urge you today to grab hold of that message – see yourself indelibly imprinted on the palm of God's hands – and be at peace, knowing you are so very loved by Him.

Dear Father, sometimes I feel so very lonely and forgotten. When these feelings overtake me, please remind me of my picture carved on the palms of Your hands. Amen

June 19
Just Do It
By Liz Anne Wright

The LORD is my light and my salvation—
whom shall I fear?
The LORD is the stronghold of my life—
of whom shall I be afraid?

Psalm 27:1 NIV

Um…Liz…there's a snake in the basement.

My dear friend and her kids were visiting and we were all preparing to go to bed. Both of us being widows, there was no man around to handle the snake problem.

I did the only thing I could do. I said a quick prayer, got a jar, and trapped the little beast.

Blessedly, it went well and it peacefully went into the jar. It was not aggressive and I did not have to chase it around the room.

It was a baby snake, about the size of a large worm.

Now, I am not overly fond of snakes, but not terribly afraid of them, either. So, I was somewhat proud of myself and told the story of my snake escapades to friends.

My friends were less than impressed.

What if there are more?

What if it had been poisonous?

What if it had bitten you?

I had, of course, thought of all these things. I just didn't see that I had a choice.

In this journey of widowhood, I am often called upon to do unexpected things, often on the spur of the moment. No time to worry. No time to shrink back or shirk my responsibilities. Just pray and do. And trust God with the results.

This somewhat humorous situation provided for me just one more example of the life lesson God has been working on with me over the past five and a half years: God's got it.

I am not really in charge; He is.

So many situations, I just have to prayerfully (often quickly) consider my options, try my best, and leave the results up to Him.

If I do that, He will be glorified.

Isn't it funny how God will take the little things in our lives to teach us big things?

I can't help but wonder if that was what is was like for David.

In service to both his earthly father and his heavenly One, David had watched the sheep, keeping them safe. I am sure he had many escapades himself. We know that he killed a lion and a bear (see 1 Samuel 17), but I am sure there were many other adventures as well. All of this seems to have been used by God as preparation for his encounter with Goliath. Not only had he developed skill with a sling that could be used there, but also a trust in God that when He gave David a task, David was capable to complete it.

Who else but I can complete the work I have been assigned?

I may be able to shrink from one task, but can I shrink from my whole life? Can I hold back when it is obvious that God has given me certain things to do?

Oh, dear sisters, I pray that you have the courage to face this journey of widowhood and whatever tasks He has set before you! The little things and the big things can all be accomplished through Him who is our glory and our strength!

Dear Father, thank You for being with me on every step of this path. Thank You for loving me enough to challenge me on this journey to grow stronger and more confident in You. Help me to feel Your love and support, Lord, as I grow in You. Help me to think on my feet when I must and slow down and wait for You when necessary. I long to glorify Your name. Help me to do that. In Your name I pray, Amen.

June 20
At the Threshold
by Katie Oldham

> *Trust in the Lord with all your heart;*
> *do not depend on your own understanding.*
> *Seek His will in all you do,*
> *and He will show you which path to take.*
> *Proverbs 3: 5-6 New Living Translation*

Remnants of my past life linger in the doorway as I stand here peering out the window into my front yard. It feels lonely here now.

We built this home together. It's where two dreams came true with the birth of our girls. I can still see him approaching in his silver truck the morning after his firefighting twenty-four hour shift. My heart yearns for the love he carried across this threshold. Nothing beat starting the day with his arrival. He always blessed our home with energy!

With anticipation I'd peek in the mirror as he approached. Call me old fashioned, but I always liked to look pretty for him! Then, I'd wipe breakfast from Stella's mouth and make sure Evelyn's diaper was clean.

I loved preparing for his warm embrace. I can almost feel his rugged hands on my back as I stand quietly here now. He'd say, "Just like a puzzle." Ahhhh…. How I miss the way we fit together.

My romantic moment deteriorated as he haphazardly chased Stella down the hallway and squawked lovingly at Evelyn leaving a mess in his path! Fast forward to now, my gaze drops from the doorway as I refocus on present time. It's all just a memory. Pre-pancreatic cancer, pre-chemo, pre-hospice, married life memories.

God, meet me in this lonely threshold! I am not sure how to keep going without Kevin ever coming home. When I hear the phone ring, I am certain it must be him. I wake in the morning sometimes forgetting he's gone.

I am left with remnants, like souvenirs from the past. When Kevin died, I so tightly held on to our life together. It was as if my knuckles turned white with fear that some part of it might slip away. My first year of widowhood was a quest to maintain status quo.. *'I can keep him alive by reliving our routines, right?'*
Denial.

'What Kevin would do in this situation? How can I recreate his presence?'
Denial.

Eventually I understood. Denial held me hostage. I had to face it! I'm a single mom now. Like it or not, my life carries on without Kevin. Our family of three needs our own identity.

Dear God, grant me the wisdom to embrace my new little family and the hope in a re-defined future.

Slowly, God started answering my prayer.

Isn't it amazing how when you finally ask God to come in, He does? He waits patiently in the thresholds of our lives until we open our hearts and let Him in.

Suddenly, I started seeing gifts and opportunities unique to my new life. I developed deeper friendships. My business started changing to better reflect my values. My involvement in my church grew, and I even began pursuing my dream to write!

God was blessing me in my new life. He empowered me to have hope through these unexpected opportunities.

You'd think I'd simply accept God's blessings with gratitude, right? No, instead my heart filled with guilt at the realization that Kevin's death offered me anything good!

Part of me wanted to dig my heels. You see, moving away from my past somehow meant moving further away from Kevin. I didn't want to loosen my grip on life with my beloved. But gradually, as I relaxed my hold on the past and held God's Word tighter, I began seeing how He could use my life's greatest loss for good.

I allowed myself to take tiny steps out on my own. I clung to God's Word in my morning devotions. I revisited my worries in evening prayers. When grief turned to frustration, I pleaded for His peace that passes all understanding. My hope in a new future grew little by little.

I started understanding that I don't have to lose Kevin's memory in order to accept God's new path for me. But, instead, He could USE that loss to create a 'me' more pleasing to Him. I started surrendering.

Dear Lord, do Your work in me. I want to see what You have in store for me!

My loss is no lighter. After two years, I still struggle with loneliness and overwhelming grief.

But, I'm learning to let the Lord mold me. I depend on Him more fervently than I ever would have known how in my past life. I am blessed beyond measure because I know more deeply the realness of His love.

Yes, it's a tough truth to swallow, knowing I savor goodness as a result of my loss. It sends pangs of pain through my heart knowing it was all planned perfectly so I could become more of the woman God wants me to be. But, I am freed from the desperate attempts at living in the past. His plans for me are good.

Dear sisters, we were not promised perfection this side of heaven's gates. Loss hurts! Set your sights on GOD's grace and allow yourself to see how you fit into His puzzle. Cling to Him for He will give you hope—hope in HIM, even when our lives didn't go as planned. We can extract lessons from our past. But rest in His embrace and surrender to His will for our futures.

Yes, Kevin, you were right. A loving embrace fits 'just like a puzzle.'

God's embrace fits for me.

Dear Father, despite the pain and sorrow of widowhood, I rejoice in the perfection of Your plan! I pray for Your wisdom. Please show me the path You place before me and guide me to lean not on my own understanding, but to walk alongside YOU. Your plans for me are GOOD! Help me to see the hope and blessings in my walk of healing. Amen.

June 21
Sisterhood of Widowhood
By Erika Graham

*But Ruth replied, "Don't urge me to leave you or to turn back
from you. Where you go I will go, and where you stay I will
stay. Your people will be my people and your God my God."*
                                                    Ruth 1:16 NIV

Recently I ran a half marathon, 13.1 crazy miles,
and my motto now is that *I am not a runner, but I do run.*
It's one of the new things God has brought into my
life, and one of the things He uses to minister to
me. Today, I wanted to share what happened during
that race that blessed me tremendously.

There were many things I experienced that day.
But the biggest surprises were the people I
encountered as I covered each mile. Some highlights
included; a man who was leading his blind wife as she
held his arm and they weaved in and out of the sea of
runners; a man, who to honor the men and women
that serve our country in the military, was in full
fatigues with boots on and a filled ruck sack strapped
to his back; a house with a DJ and a huge party going
on in the front yard as they cheered us on; and my
most favorite a sixty something year old woman
whom I shared a bond with: widowhood.

As I approached her I could see that her shirt,
like mine, was a place she chose to honor her late
husband. I ran up next to her and gave her a wink,
she saw my shirt and we gave each other a knowing
look. Then, I slowed and we ran together, exchanging
our stories. She wasn't a runner either. Her husband
passed away four years earlier. In the aftermath, she

took up running for many of the same reasons I had. As we ran, talked, shared, and encouraged each other, we realized we were in a sisterhood, a sisterhood of widowhood. We could speak a language not many can, and we had a bond and an understanding that none of my circle of close friends can share with me. Our age didn't matter, nor did our circumstances. It was such a blessing to meet her and spend just a few minutes together.

In the Bible we see wonderful sisterhoods, but my favorite now is Ruth and Naomi. Naomi had lost both her husband and awhile later her sons. Ruth was her widowed daughter-in-law. As their story unfolds, we see them become bonded together in a sisterhood of widowhood; loyal to one another, devoted, and loving. We later see God honor them, because of their deep faith in Him as well as their commitment to each other, through Ruth's marriage to Boaz. Their union produces children and grandchildren, and even a great grandson, David, who became a great King. We learn later that Jesus Christ was from the line of Ruth.

This all out of a sisterhood of widowhood!

As I reflect on this poignant story from God's Word and my journey on this widowhood road, I'm aware He's provided a wonderful network of support and encouragement for me as well. He has given widows a heart for one another, and a common bond that's created a sisterhood. We may not have signed up for this, or like it at times, but God's provisions for it are a blessing. It's a comfort to know I'm not alone in what I'm experiencing; that others have been chosen by God to walk this journey like me. Honestly, even though it's hard and I wouldn't voluntarily "choose" it, I am blessed to be in this sisterhood   of   widowhood.

Father, thank You for Your provisions for me. Even though I am in a club no one ever wants to join, and it breaks my heart to know others have to experience this too, I thank You for giving us hearts for one another. I am so blessed and grateful for the widows You have brought into my life. Lord, I pray that You will me help feel the blessings that only we can be to one another. Give me a heart to minister to others. In your matchless name, Amen.

June 22
He Sees...
by Linda Lint

> *You are El Roi – the God who sees me...*
> *Genesis 16:13 NIV*

We always knew where the other one was – my beloved and I.

It wasn't because we were possessive or controlling – it's just the way it was between us – shared lives, shared interests, the marriage covenant. He would be working in the shop, building furniture, and I could literally see him from the connecting breezeway window.

He could see me as well, and when I would sit down at the kitchen table, he would come in and join me for a break. We worked hand in hand to build our business, raise our daughter and in all the daily household tasks – even washing the dishes together!

Our lives were intricately woven together. Even after I began to work outside our home , we could mentally "see" each other. We knew the other's schedule and in our mind's eye we knew what the other was doing throughout the day.

The stroke he suffered, seven months before he passed, put him in the hospital directly across from the building where I worked at the time. I could go to my window and look upon the window to the room where he was. I knew his daily schedule then as well and what he likely was doing at any given moment.

Eventually he went to a care center. Knowing his schedule there as well, I "knew" what he was doing. He was always in "my mind's eye" and in my heart and I was in his.

In each other's hearts. That's what I miss so very, very much. I am no longer in someone's heart.

There have been days in these last two years when I have wondered if anybody sees me. Is anybody aware that I exist? Is there just one person who thinks about me on a regular basis and cares about my well-being? Of course, there are those in my life who care about me and love me. My daughter calls regularly, and there are friends who do as well. I am blessed by their love for me.

Still, there are days when in this Desert of Sorrow, I wonder.......

I think of another who found herself in a Desert of Sorrow, lost and alone. God's Word tells us about Hagar, who found herself in a desert. It was there that God met her and revealed Himself to her, letting her know He was aware of her misery. Thereafter, she referred to Him by one of His many names – El Roi – The God Who Sees Me.

And now He gently reminds me – "I am El Roi – the God who sees you".

Yes, He sees me -
When I open my eyes in the morning in bed alone.
When I leave for work and have no one to wish me a good day.
When I come home to an empty, quiet house.
When I gather the bills and the checkbook.
When I shop for one.
When I close the blinds as night falls on another day.
When I sleep.
When I sit here and type these words.
El Roi. "My God Who Sees Me."

He sees everything I do. I am in His heart, and I am always on His mind. His eyes are upon me all the time - His eyes of love, filled with tenderness towards this widow – His beloved child. I am loved beyond measure by El Roi – The One Who Sees Me.

His eyes are upon you as well, dear sister. I pray that as you read these words, you will come to know that nothing can separate you from the love of El Roi – not even the pain caused by grief. For His eyes are upon you all the time – they are the eyes of love and compassion. He knows your pain and He sees your struggle. Daily, He says "I am El Roi – I see YOU".

Dear Father, I pray that I would have a new awareness of Your love for me. I pray that I would know that You are a constant presence in my life and that You see me – that I am always on Your mind and in Your heart. Give me peace, Father. Amen

June 23
The Waiting Room
By Sherry Rickard

But they that wait upon the Lord shall renew their strength;
they shall mount up with wings as eagles;
they shall run, and not be weary;
and they shall walk, and not faint.

Isaiah 40:31 KJV

I hate waiting.

Christmas Eve to Christmas morning...doctor's appointments...test results...losing weight...shows to start...dinner to be made...grieving

I have always said, "I'm a buyer, NOT a shopper." I go in the store, find what I need, put it in the basket, walk up to the cash register, buy it, and off I go. I'm not one to put something in my cart, carry it around and think about it. In other words, I make a decision, implement it and live with the consequences...and most have been great.

When my husband was ill, we spent a lot of time in waiting rooms and in doctor examination rooms. For my husband, waiting was always the pre-cursor to bad news. The more practice I got in waiting, I forced myself to use that time to breathe and think about blessings. I would go over and over the list in my head as we waited, trying to add a blessing with each mental recitation. Eventually, the news would come; then disappointment would flood through me. My husband would thank the doctor and tell me, "It's ok, Babe, remember, it's all good!" Then we would collect our things and walk to our car as I tried to remember my mental list.

When my husband died, the whole grieving process was soooo long. As far as I could see, sadness was my companion. Endless days of what I'd lost and would never have again. No longer tables for two, but evenings with an empty chair. Waiting to feel better, happier, less lonely. Just waiting.

I found myself wanting to just leave when these feelings enveloped me. Much like Jonah, God had asked me to do something and I didn't want to. I wanted to flee. I wanted to "tap out" as they say in wrestling. Can't I have another burden? I want to have another trial, not this one. Can't God grow something else in me?

But Jonah rose up to flee... --Jonah 1:3

Much like Jonah, I found that the more I retreated from the grief "waiting room", the more grief I felt. It wasn't until I stopped running and listened to what God wanted for me that I found relief. God often speaks most clearly in life's "waiting rooms". It's when we are quiet, open, vulnerable, and ready.

I have spent some beautiful time here with God in the "waiting room". I have changed. I enjoy the wait now. I'm not so quick to just make a decision and go with it. I'm not saying I waffle in my decisions; just enjoy the process of making the decision.

I live in the Washington DC metro area. It is eighteen miles from my front door to the parking garage at work. It takes between forty minutes and two hours to get to work (one way) each workday. People say to me all the time, "Don't you just hate the commute?" I have learned to be content with where I am. If I am stuck in traffic, it must be where God needs me to be. So, I try to glorify God in my commute. I listen to music and worship Christ. I call friends and family and catch up with them to let them know they are loved. I have learned to be content in the "waiting room".

I know my grief will end at the exact moment that God has grown me to where I need to be. Each day of grief is a chance to glorify God. If I run from it, I don't grow the way God wants me to. I also don't get to leave the "waiting room".

Jonah eventually obeyed as God asked and his obedience saved many people. God has great plans for me...and you.

We won't find it by hiding from Him or hiding from the growing that He needs us to do.

Turn around, walk towards the Savior and let Him walk with you through your grief.

God may be growing you to help someone else.

Dear Lord, Thank You for allowing me time to heal and for being with me in the waiting room. Thank You for loving me enough to allow me time to grow and see the plan You have for my life. Thank You for allowing me to experience love and for knowing that love was grounded in You. I ask that You use me on this journey and that my walk through grief may be a light to someone else experiencing a similar journey. Amen

June 24
Again God, Really?
By Kathy Mills

Therefore, since we are surrounded by such a huge crowd of witnesses to the life of faith, let us strip off every weight that slows us down, especially the sin that so easily trips us up. And let us run with endurance the race God has set before us. We do this by keeping our eyes on Jesus, the champion who initiates and perfects our faith.

Hebrews 12:1-2a NLT

It will be five years this September 1, that my husband Brad died in my arms from cancer. I seriously believed after devotedly caring for, and helplessly watching the love of my life endure a prolonged and painful death, God would never have me witness that kind of loss again.

But I was wrong...

This past July 5, my eighty-five year old mom who for the past two years lived with me so I could care for her, passed into Heaven in the arms of Jesus. Her death however didn't come without a battle. I quickly realized our time together was ending when my mom's health took that giant step in its decline last month. I knew she was going to die soon since she had become bedridden. Her frail frame, weak and in constant pain desired no food and longed only for rest.

Soon our days and nights began to blend into one constant struggle to find rest. As I focused nearly every waking moment on trying to find ways to alleviate my mom's discomfort and suffering, I inwardly sensed that familiar panic and fear I had when my husband was suffering before his death. The weight of despair in my heart bore down on me and I was overwhelmed by sorrow.

I remember a couple of weeks before she died, sitting beside her bed one night. I held her hand while she slept, and prayed for God to take her now like this. I wanted her death to be peaceful and swift. I wasn't seeking His will and endurance that night...I firmly wanted mine. I couldn't imagine any good reason in the delay of her going home. I felt certain whatever God's purpose in this suffering, it could be accomplished in a better way.

These very thoughts were like the ones I had as I helplessly looked on when my husband laid suffering day and night before he died. As I became overwhelmed with the memories of my husband's long journey towards death while holding my mom's hand, my heart seemed to scream "Again God...Really?"

The Lord seemed slow to me in answering. I must admit, I felt expectant of Him to quickly remove my mom's suffering and to see things my way. He did neither.

Instead, He comforted me by revealing this; I can only hold my mom's hand for a brief visit, but He never leaves her side and is carrying her tightly to Himself. He also reminded me; while I walk in this dark valley of suffering again, I do not walk it alone. Jesus is a faithful guide, and He will never leave my side. *"Trust me"* I heard God whisper through my tears..."*remember always I am here you both.*"

I found a sweet comfort as I envisioned being tightly drawn to Jesus' side so as not to stray; walking bravely beside Him in His strength, as He gently carried my mom in His arms. Together, the three of us alone in the dark valley, feeling unafraid of the next step because God is with me. I felt covered in His peace.

I don't know why God allowed my husband and mom to suffer so greatly before leaving this life to be with Him. I also don't know why God would have me experience their last days, feeling helpless in their suffering. I may never know this side of Heaven the good it brought or His purpose fulfilled, which could have been accomplished "a better way" as I often think it could. Thankfully, God doesn't ask me to understand...He simply asks, *"Do you trust me?"* What else can I answer but, *"Yes Lord, I trust you."*

Today like many other days, I miss my husband...and I miss my mom & dad too. The three people who mattered most to me are all gone from my life now. I hold in my spirit that great hope and comfort in knowing I'll see them again one day in Heaven...but that doesn't mean I don't have days like today when I just plain want to see them...now! There have been many times when unexpectedly the deepest pain hits, leaving me feeling empty and gasping for *"something more...something better"* than what I feel I've been left with.

Sometimes the very thought of having many more years here without them can be quite depressing...until I stop looking at my future as I see it through what has been lost. Instead, I'd rather see my future through God's promises and believe God's Word which say His plans for my future are good and my life will not end without His good and loving purpose being fulfilled. I'd rather live expectantly & with anticipation of what God has in store for my future days than live them out in dread and defeat. Just writing that makes me smile at the thought of death's sting losing some of its power over me.

What about you? Will you join me and set your eyes on Jesus too as we run this race called life together?

You know...after trials of sorrow like this one, I even think I can hear my husband's voice among a distant cheering crowd. As I endure another lap of grief, with my eyes and thoughts fixed on Jesus, I keep running towards the finish line with Him.

Victory in Jesus...it's already mine.

And He said to me, 'My grace is sufficient for you, for My strength is made perfect in weakness.' Therefore most gladly I will rather boast in my infirmities, that the power of Christ may rest upon me.

2 Corinthians 12:9 NKJV

June 25
A Moment With God in My Kitchen
By Kit Hinkle

Do not be anxious about anything, but in everything by prayer and petition, with thanksgiving, present your requests to God.
Philippians 4:6 NIV

Do people tell you you're doing great, but secretly you feel like you're going from day to day--hour to hour, feeling overwhelmed? Having friends, but feeling like your friends don't really get you?

It's okay—you're not alone. Want to know the truth? Even non-widows feel this way. Being a widow simply means we can at least put a name to our adversity and share in a community to support one another.

Still, the adversity of having lost someone really special in your heart is one that just doesn't go away. And the trials along with moving forward without him don't go away.

And then...

There are moments of peace. They usually come when God or someone points out how well you are doing—or moments when you help another in distress and realize how far you have come.

Like when my teens had a sleepover the other night, and I heard them stirring downstairs in the morning. "Are you guys ready for breakfast?" I asked.

"After we finish part six," they called back.

Part six? Are they playing a video game? "Part six of what?" I asked.

"Of the Bible!" they shouted back.

"Part six of the Bible?" I asked. "What's that?"

"No--not part six," they laughed. "Mark 6".

They had woken up and on their own decided to read the Bible together.

That's a wink from the Lord. For that moment, all anxiety--gone.

Peace came and hung out with me for a while.

And then, the air conditioning broke.

It's Sunday morning, the house is hot, and I'm supposed to go to worship, but the thought of replacing the ac and the thousands it will cost and the repair men I will have to haggle with just overwhelmed me. In itself, this wouldn't unnerve me, but I had recently been obsessing over my finances, having had to replace a car because the engine blew up and helping my oldest plan for college with no funds to pay for it.

The combination of concerns had me sitting alone in my kitchen aching with anxiety, then turning it over to Him, then taking it back into a dull ache, then trying again to give it to Him—over and over. I made the calls to the AC service company. I prayed and wept. Thoughts about the wealthy man I turned down in marriage crept in, and then I remember that the Lord steered me away from that choice for good reason, and reminded me of that yesterday with my boys reading His Word.

As I quietly breathed through these cycles of worry and release to the Lord in my kitchen, the phone rang.

It was my neighbor, Louis. "I wanted to let you know I heard your AC motor sounding bad, so I shut it off from the outside. It's probably a fan motor. I just had my entire AC in my house replaced and I have the old equipment under the house, so if the repair man says you need new parts, just know I have them and you won't need to buy the parts."

Another moment.

Thank you, God. You **are** there. Every step. I won't be discouraged, and I will run the race fully.

These moments are gifts. They are glimpses of Heaven—of Truth. They remind us we have purpose in this season. Thank you, Lord, for Your encouragement, because we must keep our joy through our struggles!

Sister, remind yourself that we as widows aren't the only ones who struggle. There comes that point in everyone's life, when you experience first-hand how empty the promises of the world are.

It's not that the world is all bad, and there is so much beauty here too—but you somehow start to recognize that true joy, true contentment cannot come from our circumstances.

That's when you thank God that He offers something eternal for us to hope for.

And you brush off the pain and move forward--every day-- just focusing on what's in front of you, never letting anxiety stop you.

One day I will go Home, knowing this world offers nothing for me.

But meanwhile I enjoy what beauty there is here to enjoy, and honor God by living each day here--an alien in this world-- looking to do my Father's will.

June 26
Get Back Up...
By Nancy Howell

I'm guessing my nine year old brought it home a week ago last Saturday. "It" being the flu, influenza B to be exact. Up to this point, my sons had made it through the school year relatively untouched by sickness--no runny noses, viruses, or flu to speak of.

That run of good luck ended on Sunday as the boy started running fever, having head and body aches, and respiratory manifestations...only twenty-four hours after attending a city-wide pancake festival with his Big Brother. My symptoms began on Tuesday morning, with the final holdout, the eleven year old, succumbing late Tuesday night. All three of us, hit square between the eyes with the flu.

It was awful. None of us felt like doing anything. Laundry, cleaning, even simple tasks like unloading the dishwasher took a level of strength we didn't possess. Making sure we all took our medicine, ate a bit of food every once in a while, and taking care of the two cats and the dog was about all this mama could muster for three to four days.

I missed my helpmate, my better half for over twenty years, in a way I hadn't experienced since his death, over eighteen months ago.

This widow thing can sure be hard at times. Just whenever I think I have a handle on what it takes to be a single parent, raising two sons on my own, I get a reality check. I think I'm coping, making progress on the day-to-day tasks at hand, and then a little thing like the flu knocks me flat on my backside, bringing my momentum to a screeching halt.

Not feeling like doing much of anything, I retreated to my huge bed, with its snuggly flannel sheets and electric blanket. Sometimes just doing nothing is the best medicine of all. While nestled under the covers, I heard it. "It" this time being a still small voice, both authoritative and undeniable. And boy, did I ever listen.

"Nancy, you have been putting off doing _____, what for over seven months now? What's the deal? You know I need you to do this. It will help My kingdom here on earth."

"Lord, I'm sorry. I've been busy. Between raising the boys, keeping the house running, going to practices and piano lessons, grocery shopping, financial planning, yada-yada-yada, the time just seems to slip away."

"Well, it looks like you have the perfect time now. You're not doing anything else."

"But I'm sick. My head feels like it is going to explode. I have two sick boys, a house that looks like a tornado's been afoot, and so many chores piling up that it makes me want to cry."

"Child, have you ever thought of asking Me for help? Seems here lately you're trying to do this all on your own. You know better. Remember back whenever you could not take one step without Me holding your hand or carrying you? We are an unstoppable team. Just because you think you can do it without Me doesn't mean you should attempt such nonsense. With My help, we can accomplish wondrous things in your life, all of it for My glory!"

Now maybe it was a bit of delirium caused by fever, but I think otherwise. God didn't make me sick, but He sure used the opportunity to get a word or two (or hundred) in with me.

God shouldn't have to wait for a time whenever I'm down or sick with the flu to get my attention. He deserves my attention and praise and worship at all times....24/7/365.

We ended up having a productive chat, my Master and I. He's so wonderfully forgiving, and He fills me up to overflowing with love, praise, and happiness. If I just give Him a bit of time.

The Tamiflu finally did the job. The three Howells are up and around, playing catch-up on mundane tasks such as class work, housework, and going a week without exercise. Physical healing is a wonderful thing. But oh-so-much better is the spiritual healing, the reality check God gave me while I was flat on my back.

We fall back down, we get back up again. And again. And again. And again.

And after you suffer for a short time, God, who gives all grace, will make everything right. He will make you strong and support you and keep you from falling. He called you to share in his glory in Christ, a glory that will continue forever.
1 Peter 5:10 NCV

Dear friends, God doesn't care how many times we fail Him. He's the one that created us, gave us free will, so He expects us to get distracted at times with the tasks at hand. But each one of us has a purpose, a God-given reason for living--it's just up to us to figure out the details. And the only way we can discern what He wants from us and what He wants to do through us is to give Him our time.

Did you ever think that maybe the situation you are in now is the reality check for the purpose God has for you?

We lose our way...we get back up again. It's never too late to get back up again. You may be knocked down, but not out forever....

Get up, you beautiful, lovely creation of God's own hand. You've got work to do.

He'll give you the strength if you give Him the time.

<u>June 27</u>
Leftovers
By Danita Hiles

The results of the word study flashed across my computer screen. Somehow seeing it in black and white made it seem more real than just hearing it out loud:

Wid-ow (n) : A woman (of any age) who has lost her husband by death and has not remarried.

Or-phan (n) : a child who has lost both parents through death.

Widow. Orphan. Apparently I am both. (cue tiny violins for one minute pity party)

Sigh. Neither one of these are labels I would have chosen for this season of my life.

But did you know these words also have other meanings? In editing, the terms 'widow' and 'orphan' are used for those couple of extra words or letters which are left over at the end of a page or paragraph when formatting for print.

Extra. Leftover. The bits that don't fit on the page. Sound familiar?

The extra 'manless' female at a gathering of well-meaning friends.

The 'left over' ones when everyone at Disney walks by in perfect family groupings.

The "bits that just don't fit" when folks are seated two-by-two at celebrations or soccer games or graduation ceremonies.

It catches me by surprise at times, this slightly awkward feeling of not fitting.

Thankfully, God's word has a lot to say on the subject. I love the way that He singles these two groups out by name, maybe because in the 'left-outness' of life, He knows we need a little bit of special attention. Here is His perspective:

Psalm 68:5-6 NIV A father to the fatherless, a defender of widows, is God in his holy dwelling. God sets the lonely in families, he leads out the prisoners with singing;

In editing, when there are widows and orphans at the end of the page, the page needs to be re-formatted so that the extra words will fit in place. Seems to me, the same principle works within my circumstances. And yours.

The life I **have**, is not the life I **had**. And I can't expect it to look or feel the same. Maybe it's time for some creative reformatting, God style.

Plan - For holidays and special events, one of the best ways to avoid the awkward is to have a plan. Easter dinner at my house is no longer family dinner with all the fixings and a fancy table. Last year we chose to pack up ham sandwiches and head to the beach. It's whatever works for your little family.

Reach out - No matter how deep your sadness, you can always find someone to reach out to. I love to invite a bunch of other folks who feel 'left over' to my house. Fancy is not important. Folks simply love to be invited. Back to Psalm 68. 'He sets the lonely in families'. This is so true! I am so blessed with all the 'faux family' friends who have embraced the girls and I over the years!

Get creative – Entertaining used to feel a little weird, especially if I invited a couple and their kids, because the husband always felt like the lone ranger. Now, I invite two couples that I think would hit it off and everybody has a great time.

Trust - Sometimes, it just is what it is. And whether you are the lone parent clapping wildly at your child's performance or simply sitting alone in church, you can smile quietly with the knowledge of His promises tucked away in your heart.

*Joshua 1:5 NIV No one will be able to stand against you all the days of your life. As I was with Moses, so **I will be with you**; I will never leave you nor forsake you.*

Ok friends, how about you? Have you found any clever ways to 'reformat' your way of doing life during this walk through the valley?

June 28
Every Star
By Julie Wright

He determines the number of stars and calls them each by name. Great is the Lord and mighty in power, his understanding has no limit.
Psalm 147:4-5 NIV

We just returned from a fabulous summer vacation visiting family in North Carolina. We spent two weeks rafting, taking evening walks, gobbling up the fresh blackberries off the trail, and watching for fireflies in the woods.

We'd enjoy our dinners out on the porch listening to the waterfall and comical family chats and stories while hummingbirds buzzed past our heads. Amongst all the jammed packed adventure and family fun, I needed some quiet time for myself. I knew that I needed some time alone to renew my mind and spirit. My parents graciously agreed to watch the kids for a bit so that I could re-charge.

It wasn't that I didn't want to spend every moment I could with my family, but the daily duties of being a single mom wear on me, if I'm honest. Sometimes I feel like running away or shipping the kids off to my parents for a few weeks just so I can breathe. Don't get me wrong. I love my kids. I'm honored to be there mom. It's just that occasionally I get in a pile of pity and wallow around with my giant "W" on my chest for widow. I figure this isn't what I signed up for when I took my vows. It shouldn't have to be this way.

So, I slipped away one evening out to the deck for some peace and quiet. All that could be heard were the katydids humming a joyful tune in the darkness. I sat on the deck with tears falling down my face and wondering how Satan could have such a stronghold on me still. How could he subtly creep in and rob me of the joy and happiness I should be feeling?

I began to pray. Asking God to help me let go. To help me live in the here and now. To give me some peace, some comfort, some sign that He hears me. That He cares about me still. That He hadn't forgotten about this sad, lonely widow.

I sat in silence for a few minutes. The katydids didn't even make a peep. They were probably terrified that I was about to feel the wrath of God for being so bold to ask Him such things. A gentle breeze blew across my face. I opened my eyes and looked up at the heavens. The sky was pitch black and the stars twinkled so brightly and clearly. It felt as though I could reach up and pluck them from the sky. A smile crossed my face and the words to one of my favorite songs came to mind.

He numbers each and every star and calls them all by name.

Every star...every star. Scientists estimate that there are one hundred thousand million stars in the Milky Way and millions upon millions in other galaxies. But I still matter more to Him. He loves me right where I am. Valley or mountain top, He loves me the same.

Nothing can separate me from His love. Not death. Not sadness. Not fear. Not loneliness. Not the stresses of motherhood. Nothing can keep Him from loving me.

How about you, sweet sisters? Do you struggle with believing you matter? That he hears and sees you?

Will you join me this week in the backyard hammock staring at the evening sky and thanking Him for seeing right where we are? I'll say a prayer for you for every star I see. Will you do the same for me?

June 29
Earthly Treasures
By Karen Emberlin

But godliness with contentment is great gain.
For we brought nothing into the world,
and we can take nothing out of it.
1 Timothy 6:6-7 NIV

For fifteen months my husband and I lived in a suburban neighborhood in the comfort of a three bedroom home with a finished basement, double car garage, and attic.

We were normal. In other words, like most Americans, our home was "filled" with all of the "stuff" we had collected over forty-eight years of marriage. Even after moving several times during those years, we always took our "stuff" with us, sure we would eventually need it.

Things changed! Once I lost my husband, that "stuff" we thought was so valuable no longer seemed valuable, and I realized the only real value it ever had was because it was "ours". What good would that do me now?

Overnight all of my "stuff" became a real burden.

The unexpected loss had my relatives and me scratching our heads--where would I go? And what would I do with all these things?

First I relocated to another state to be with our daughter and family. With no room for a house full of my stuff, my daughter asked me to downsize. And I did--from a three bedroom house to the twenty-two foot trailer I used to move to Florida.

In order to reduce my treasure to what fit in that twenty-two foot trailer, I sorted. I don't remember where it all ended up, but I was always happy when someone I knew took an item I may have had a hard time letting go of. At least I knew where its new home would be!

As my son and I pulled away from my home, I thought about the trailer we were towing behind us. My husband had bought it a few years earlier for a "local" move, so we could take our time. I had always thought it to be in the way. "Let's sell it," I'd say. "Nah," he'd say, 'Someday we might need it!"

In God's perfect plan, He knew I'd be the one who would need it. That trailer "housed" my treasures for a whole year.

While living with less at my daughter's home. I discovered how comfortable I was with just a very small amount of my belongings around me.

But God wasn't done pruning my earthly treasures.

A few months ago I moved yet again--this time over a thousand miles away, to a community with an even smaller space to fit my belongings. Faced again with the decisions of getting my "stuff", I began again the process of sorting and deciding what was really important, this time placing my "stuff" in a 5x8 U-haul trailer.

From a house to a twenty-two footer to a 5x8 trailer--God's forcing me to adjust my definition of success.

It was not easy to "let go" of things that I once thought were so important, especially some of the things that my husband enjoyed so much (like the cargo trailer)!

However, as I made those choices, I was reminded that my husband left this world with none of our "stuff", and I too will leave without it. He has so much more in his heavenly home than we ever had here!!

Yes, I miss my husband so much, and I want to be comfortable and have some of the things we enjoyed together near me. I have been able to do that.

Best of all, I have a heart full of memories, and love that I do not ever have to "give up"!

I realize that by not having the burden of moving, storing, or caring for so many things, I am freeing myself to be all I can for the Lord and can prepare myself for the plans He has for me.

He promises to give me hope and a future (even without my husband). I want to be ready to follow wherever He takes me, and am excited to see what is next!

Lord, I pray that You will be with me on this journey when it is difficult to give up "earthly treasures". Help me to find contentment in You and to store up "heavenly treasures" that will be waiting for me when I get to my home with You. Amen

June 30
Not Intimidated!
By Kit Hinkle

Don't hold back—you're not going to come up short. You'll forget all about the humiliations of your youth, and the indignities of being a widow will fade from memory.
Isaiah 54:4 The Message

When I worked in the corporate world, I had a friend who was a mover and a shaker. By now, I'm quite sure Ed is a CEO somewhere in this universe.

Ed's motto was don't ask permission. Do what you've got to do and apologize for it later! He wasn't a rule breaker, but Ed found success at every corner because people knew whatever he touched was going to get done and in a big way.

When my youngest was eight, he had the same motto. He asked me to take him to a local theme park to ride a roller coaster called The Intimidator. Never mind that he was about four inches shy of the height requirement! Even standing as tall as he could with every trick in the book—tall Healey roller shoes that add about an inch, and two hats stacked tall on his head, the park official who measured him sadly shook his head while choking back a laugh.

But Christian didn't give up. He went to Top Gun next, and then the BORG Assimilator—two of the biggest coasters in the park. Every time a park official with a big measuring stick shook his head, Christian smiled and stepped away, undaunted.

"You'll just have to eat your green vegetables," I said.

Christian became a connoisseur of snap peas and carrots. "I'll keep trying," he said. "If I keep trying, someone will think I'm tall enough."

I thought about Christian and Ed.

Then I thought about us ladies who have to take on life with unexpected challenges, like doing it alone when you thought you'd always have your husband by your side.

Sometimes, I think the world expects us to fold, to ask permission for steps we have to take to move forward. I suppose I don't think so, I know so. I remember a decision I made a year after Tom died. I chose to build a sun porch for the boys and me.

I had a close friend question me on it. She worried over my decision to spend the money, and took it upon herself to discuss it among our circle of friends. It shook me up for a bit, not because I wondered whether my decision was sound, but because I wondered whether our friendship could endure her criticism. It's a sad reality, but some friendships don't survive when you lose your husband. When you move forward as head of the household, you might find friends and loved ones unaccustomed to seeing you take on that role. But you can't hide behind a husband anymore. You have to become your own mover and shaker.

So I built the sun porch without anyone's permission but God's. And guess what? He blessed it. I didn't even have to apologize for it later! I've had it for years now, and the boys love it. We have it wired with a flat screen and a DVD and it becomes movie central for the kids in the neighborhood on summer nights. I consider it one of the best decisions we made in these years without Tom.

Lord, Please continue to guide me as I lean on You for direction. When I seek permission, let it be You and only You I seek it from. Help me to have the courage to act on Your guidance and not worry about the crowd. Amen

July

July 1
Memories
By Elizabeth Dyer

> *The memory of the righteous will be a blessing...*
> *but love covers all wrongs."*
> *Proverbs 10:7, 12 NIV*

What do you do with those memories? You know the ones. How do you reconcile the painful with the wonderful? Why is it that the hardest ones come most easily to our memories?

As I was reading in Proverbs this morning, God highlighted several verses for me to meditate on. "The memory of the righteous will be a blessing". But who are the righteous? Those without sin? Those who never strayed from the straight and narrow? The Bible teaches us that the righteous are the ones who are "right" before God. And that only happens because of the work of Jesus Christ on the cross, dying for our sins and rising again, conquering death.

So does that mean a husband who sinned can be remembered as righteous? Let's hope so!

We all sin!! (Romans 3:23) How do I remember the husband who committed suicide or had addictions or anger issues? Is there any hope of his being remembered as righteous? Thankfully God doesn't allow anyone into heaven based on their last sin or their last good deed. We would all be in trouble if He did. We are only allowed into heaven based on Christ's work, nothing that we do on our own. (Ephesians 2:8,9)

My challenge today is allowing "love to cover all wrongs". Especially in my marriage. I found a letter yesterday in my husband's files. It was written before we were married, to our best friend (who lived in another state) and me (also living elsewhere). He had copied it, not sure why. But it was a gift. A gift from God to remind me of the man I fell in love with. The man I couldn't wait to marry. The man I enjoyed spending time with for five years as my best friend before we said, "I do". The man who could apply Scripture to just about any situation.

Fast forward a couple decades. We had some unexpected events in our marriage that took our lives down a path I never would have imagined. How do I look at him and see "memories of the righteous"? That is a daily struggle. Hourly. Satan brings to mind all the "dirty laundry". Satan wants me to think his sins were worse than my own. Satan wants me to be bitter and angry. Satan wants me to see my husband as unrighteous instead of righteous.

God allowed the readers of Scripture to peak into the lives of many of His children and we see the good, the bad, and the ugly. We see murder. Sexual sins. Lying. Deceit. Drunkenness. Insecurity. Impatience. These people we read about were flawed. What hope! God didn't hold those sins against them – He had them listed in the chapter of the faithful (Hebrews 11).

Love. It covers all wrongs. God's love. My love. Your love. It can change the way you remember your spouse. It doesn't change the events, though. And I have to look at him through "grace glasses" and not judgment. I have to remember he is forgiven and complete in Christ.

He understood grace in a way I may never understand it. I sometimes still think that somehow I DESERVE salvation, that I am a pretty good person because I am not like someone else! That is judgment, not grace, my friend. Nothing in me deserves salvation. God's grace and love covers my heart and makes me presentable before God's throne.

As a concrete reminder to look at my late husband through grace glasses, I have chosen to wear his wedding ring on my left hand. I removed my wedding band and placed his ring on my middle finger. I hope to be reminded of God's grace in my life each time I notice it there on my hand. That is my reminder each day. And hopefully I can allow God to bring good memories of a righteous man to my mind and see God's love and my own love for him covering the rest of the memories.

Dear Father God, Thank You for my husband. He was flawed and sinful but loved by You. Give me enough love to cover those memories that need to be covered. And give me the blessing of the good memories. Don't let me stay in the memories of his mistakes but address them and move on. Your grace is sufficient for every memory. Remind me of my need for Your grace in my life every day. Thank You for Your grace. Amen

July 2
A Love So Deep
By Leah Stirewalt

Within one week of my husband's death, I returned to blogging again. Some might find that rather strange and untimely. For me...very therapeutic. As a lover of words, yet unable to form many with my mouth during those early weeks, I turned to my other passion...writing. I kept a journal (and still do) but find most of my thoughts then (and now) get poured out on my personal blog site.

Shockingly, a new world opened up for me. One that I was completely oblivious to before my husband's suicide. I began receiving blog comments, email messages, Facebook comments, and even Twitter love – mostly aimed at encouraging me through the darkest days I'd ever experienced in my thirty-nine years. Even more, I became acquainted with strangers – many of whom I now call friends – that are also widows themselves (some even by suicide). I began to realize I wasn't alone. I knew I wasn't the only one that had walked the same road. But, I also knew I needed some help and certainly couldn't do this alone.

This grief journey is not for the faint at heart. The tough, independent woman of yesteryear no longer seemed to be around. I found myself quite needy actually – a word I never associated myself with before. I went through the motions of living each day, but I couldn't accomplish much more than that. Decision making? Virtually impossible. Food prep? Forget about it. House cleaning? I couldn't care less.

Nevertheless, I was blessed with an army of helpmates to fill in the gaps. Friends from church, co-workers, neighbors, family, and even complete strangers became my angels of mercy. God poured out His comfort on us in amazing ways through His children. I will never forget that tremendous blessing in those early weeks.

A month passed. Life started to become "real" again. Deep loneliness set in. I found myself seeking that "help" again. *Anyone out there?* I couldn't expect people to continue to lavish personal attention upon us forever, but I wasn't ready for it to end so abruptly. In all actuality, it didn't end. We're still being cared for (eight months later) in some rather amazing ways, but the huge saturation of daily care did stop. And, I really understood that. People have lives to live outside of serving new Widow Leah and her daughter. I just wasn't ready for it.

It was then God's voice became quite loud to me. He wanted to be the center of my need. And, in the stillness of our times together, He spoke frequently to my heart.

Am I enough daughter?

If I take it all away…will you still return to Me?

Can you trust Me to care for you completely?

Do you know how massive My love is for you?

"Yes Lord! Of course! You are enough. I'll always return to You. Of course I trust you, and I know You love me deeply."

But, He wouldn't stop. I don't think He was satisfied with my answer. Maybe because it was what I thought He wanted to hear.

I know your heart, Leah. Remember, I crafted it. You can hide nothing from Me.

Again, am I enough? Will you always return to Me? Can you completely trust Me? Do you know the depth of My love?

"OK, Father. You want the truth. Here it goes… I say You're enough, but I haven't lost all yet. Chris wasn't my everything, but he was pretty close. I say I'll always return to You. Lord, I pray that to always be true. I can't imagine life without You. But, if I don't stay near to You, I'm sure even I can develop a wandering heart. Please protect me from ever wandering from You sweet Lord!

As for trusting…I need You to really help me with this one. I have nobody to fully trust but You, but I'm struggling here Lord. How's that for honesty? You're the only One I can always trust and yet I'm struggling to do just that. What's wrong with me?"

I can tell you what's wrong, my beloved daughter. You don't understand the depth of My love for you. And, you never fully will understand it completely this side of paradise, but allow Me to show you as much as you will open your physical eyes to see. Even more of My love will be shown to you through your eyes of faith. And one day daughter…one blessed day…your faith will become your sight! Until that day, rest Leah…rest in Me! I want to carry all of your pain, because I love you completely!

Read the paragraph above again, this time make it a prayer from your heart.

July 3
Garden Delight
By Julie Wright

> *They will be like a tree planted by the water*
> *that sends out its roots by the stream.*
> *It does not fear when heat comes;*
> *its leaves are always green.*
> *It has no worries in a year of drought*
> *and never fails to bear fruit."*
>
> Jeremiah 17:8 NIV

I love to sit out on my patio doing a morning devotion and take in all the wonderful creations from God. I can see all the new growth on the trees, bulbs peeking up from the earth, and hear the birds singing melodic tunes through the air and the feeling evoked from all this "newness" is a happy, content feeling, that life is just good.

Since we have moved to our new home, we have been so busy fixing things and trying to organize box after box that I haven't had time to think about the state of our yard much. My daughter has been faithfully nagging me about our garden. At our "old" house, we gardened together all the time. We planted sunflower seeds each fall and we wrote out the word "LOVE" for Christmas in impatiens. I love to garden with her. She notices all the little things that I sometimes take for granted. The sprout of carrot that is just barely peeking through the soil. The tiny worm wiggling around and helping our plants get "really big." So, after a few weeks of hearing her wishing about our new garden, we went shopping. We decided to tackle a small veggie and herb garden first.

We hit the store and got all the veggies and herbs that we liked the best and a few for brother too. We prepped our soil. We made sure all the rocks were gone and we added in a really nice brick border. We carefully mapped out our plan and then we started putting in our plants and seeds. Sheer delight was across both of our faces as we stood back and enjoyed our hard work after giving our new garden a good, long drink of cool water.

The next morning, she was the first one up and headed out to see how things were "growing." She watered everything again. She informed me that things were looking good and I needed to be patient. God would take care of it for us.

She was right. Within a few short days our green beans peeked out along with some lettuce, carrots and cucumbers. The tomatoes and herbs were happily stretching up toward the warm sun as well.

It has now been a little while since we planted our garden and blooms are everywhere. We have blossoms on our peppers, blueberries, cucumbers and beans. Our tomatoes have nice green fruit on almost every branch. We can't wait to partake.

Now, what on earth does this story have to do with widowhood? It's simple. We are all like the seeds or small plantings that we so carefully took care of and watched over. As widows, we need to be sure that our "roots" remain close to God and planted in good soil (His Word) so that we will have a firm and deep foundation when the thunderstorms come our way.

I think of our tears as the rain water that the plants need for growth.

It says in Revelations that He will wipe every tear from us. He knows our sorrow. He understands our sorrow. He allows those tears to flow as part of the healing and growth that we need to keep drawing ourselves closer to Him.

I think of the fertilizer used to help bring some strength and extra nutrients to the new growth and plants as our friends. Those people who have come along side of us and prayed with us. Held our hands. Brought us meals. Provided for us monetarily or through gifts. Those who have just sat and listened with us or offered that hug or smile that we desperately craved in those long, lonely days, weeks or months.

And finally the sun. Plants need the sun for warmth and growth and quite frankly, we need the Son, for the exact same reasons. The Son comforts us in those deep, dark valleys and reminds us that the Sonlight, ALWAYS overcomes the darkness. The Son helps us grow in our faith and in our beliefs that there is more to this life here on earth. The Son makes us look up. In order to see that goodness and feel that warmth, our faces need to be turned to Him, just like the leaves in our garden.

My prayer is that you will plant your roots deep in His Word. Cry the tears of healing and growth whenever you need to. Reach out to your friends and allow them to be the fertilizer that you need them to be. But, most importantly, don't take your eyes off of the Son. He's always "tending" to you, whether you feel Him or not, He's our ultimate gardener.

July 4
To Everything There Is A Season
By Nancy Howell

There is a time for everything,
and everything on earth has its special season.
There is a time to be born
and a time to die.
There is a time to plant
and a time to pull up plants.
There is a time to cry
and a time to laugh.
There is a time to be sad
and a time to dance.
There is a time to throw away stones
and a time to gather them.
There is a time to hug
and a time not to hug.
There is a time to look for something
and a time to stop looking for it.
There is a time to keep things
and a time to throw things away.
Ecclesiastes 3:1-2,4-6 NCV

Today is my birthday. It's a big one, my fiftieth. In the days leading up to this, I have been reflecting on past birthdays. A few have stood out from the rest:

- My tenth: turning a whole decade seemed monumental at the time.

- My twenty-fifth: the most memorable up to that time. My husband proposed on my quarter century celebration, and life as I knew it would never be the same!
- My thirtieth: celebrated at my new job, in my new home state, Texas, surrounded by a host of friends and coworkers.
- My fortieth: celebrated on the final day of my last full-time job. I was seven months pregnant with my second son, my first only fifteen months old at the time.

And now, here I sit, on my fiftieth. I'm not in the season I expected. I am a widow of almost two years, single mother to an eleven and nine year old. Not where I thought I would be.

Are any of us where we "thought we would be" at this particular point in our lives?

There are seasons to life. Solomon, the author of Ecclesiastes puts it so beautifully..."*there is a time for everything, and everything on earth has a special season...*"

If you are reading this, you are most likely a widow, or someone who is acquainted with a widow.

Of all the seasons of my life thus far, this one, thrust upon me in July of 2011, is the most unwanted. 48 year old happily-married women don't become widows, do they? God doesn't allow young boys, ages 8 and 9, to become suddenly fatherless, does He?

"Happily ever after?"

In my case, it ended way too soon.

Re-read the passage at the beginning of today. Listen to what God puts on your heart. Tomorrow we will look at what God showed me in our passage. When you read through it again today, jot down some ideas that jump out to you. Then we can compare notes.

<u>July 5</u>
To Everything There is a Season Continued
By Nancy Howell

Yesterday I began telling you about my fiftieth birthday and how I wasn't supposed to be a widow with young kids. I read an Old Testament passage that really spoke to me. Here's what God showed me about Ecclesiastes chapter 3:

There is a time to be born and a time to die. Only God knows those times. Mere humans cannot grasp nor fathom, God's mind nor His timing.

There is a time to plant and a time to pull up plants. A season of putting down roots, of growing children and relationships. A season to find the strength to cut ties and move forward.

There is a time to cry and a time to laugh. Praise God, those times can be simultaneous. Women, I think, are particularly versed in this anomaly. In my situation, I hope for much more laughing than crying.

There is a time to be sad and a time to dance. Sad times? Oh friends, we all have them. My season of sadness is finally transforming into a season of dancing, but it has taken months of God's unfailing grace to heal me. A widow cannot sit on the sidelines and not actively pursue healing. You must do the work to reap the benefits, so that your time of sadness isn't the end of your story here on earth.

There is a time to hug, and a time not to hug. Another translation phrases it, " a time to embrace and a time to refrain." I've personally never turned down a hug, nor the chance to give one. But there are instances in life where we should embrace people and circumstances, and times where we should show restraint.

There is a time to look for something, and a time to stop looking for it. There are times that searching for something in particular can be a positive thing. But some things we look for, we will never find...in those times, God wants us to stop and move on.

There is a time to keep things, and a time to throw things away. What things in your life are most precious to you? Take inventory--some are precious and should be kept. Others may be extra, non-necessary, and can be thrown away. We may find we don't need many of the "things" in life that we thought made us happy.

God has a plan for each life. In each, we are given seasons, cycles of time where there's work for us, lessons to be learned. As flawed humans, it is easy to question God's plan and His timing, especially whenever our lives don't turn out the way we envision them.

I could have resented God allowing me to become a widow. *I chose not to*.

I could have cursed Him for leaving my sons without an earthly daddy, the best man I have ever had the privilege of knowing---*but I did not*.

I may have entered this current season of my life reluctantly, practically kicking and screaming on July 30, 2011--but time, wisdom, and hindsight have allowed me to see that God can weave His beauty even into the saddest of seasons.

I believe the secret to having peace is this: each of us must discover, accept, and appreciate God's timing. We must choose to believe that it is perfect, regardless of what the world tells us.

And never, ever forget--this is not the end of the story. We're merely in a dress rehearsal for eternity, where God wins. There and only there, we'll finally understand the seasons we've been given on this side of heaven.

To everything, turn, turn, turn...

Dear Heavenly Father, I approach Your throne today with thanksgiving in my heart. Thank You for allowing me to celebrate many years on this earth. I have seen many seasons of my life thus far. I pray that You will continue to reveal Your plan for me, especially on days that I struggle with my current circumstances. I pray that I will put my trust totally in You and in Your perfect timing. In Jesus' name I ask it all, Amen.

Take heart, dear sisters, in whatever season of life you are in--you are not alone. It is my birthday wish that each of you find peace in God's timing.

July 6
Hear Me!
By Erika Graham

> *Whoever has ears, let them hear.*
> *Matthew 11:15 NIV*

My son, Ben, often hears half of what is said, or he hears what's said and misinterprets it. One time while driving, my other two children made a comment about a dead raccoon on the side of the road. Ben only heard two words, "raccoon" and "day', in their comments. So he piped up with this question, "Wait, is it raccoon day?"

Another time we were at a store when Ben proclaimed he needed to go to the bathroom. I begged him to hold it until I finished shopping and we had made our way through the check-out line. A few minutes later he was adamant he couldn't wait, so I told him he needed to pinch his cheeks and just hang in. He reached up with both his hands and pinched the cheeks on his face. I began to laugh and explain I meant his other cheeks. So he reached down and pinched those with his hands as well. He looked at me confused wondering how this might possibly help. Needless to say, that is one of my all-time favorite stories and it leads to a very fun and interesting conversation about pinching and squeezing cheeks.

When my husband passed away I wrestled with God. One of my biggest questions was why He hadn't heard us. I saw my husband's death as a failure on God's part to hear our cry of heartfelt prayers beseeching Him to help us.

As I searched His word, He reminded me of His promises. You see I realized I was misinterpreting everything I was hearing, just like my Benny boy does sometimes. I took my husband's tragic death and assumed that I had it figured out. I assumed I could hear by what I was seeing.

In the Bible, fifteen times in the New Testament, the authors write "Whoever has ears, let him hear". Jesus says it eight times and the book of Revelation says it seven more times. It seems obvious it's rather important for us to use our ear to hear. But, I was using my eyes to hear. I saw the pain I was in, and the suffering my children and our family and friends were enduring. I SAW the impact and devastation his sudden death had on us!

But, once I opened myself up to "close" my eyes and HEAR with my ear, God's word poured out over me. "I know the plans I have for you, plans to prosper you..." "I can do all things through Christ..." "Healing comes in the..." "I have overcome death..." "He who believes in me…" "He works all things for his glory and our good…"

Healing! My revelation came- Lord, you did heal my husband. The Bible tells us "nothing separates us from You", so I know he's in Your presence in his heavenly form, fully healed. You did answer our prayers, but it was definitely not in the way we prayed, and certainly not in the way we envisioned.

As time passes, peace has washed over me, and I have now found a deeper resolve and understanding to better enable me to hear what God is revealing. I'm also comforted by His promises to not only hear my prayers, but to faithfully answer them. I've seen Him answer so many prayers throughout my life, before and after my husband's passing; sometimes similar to what I prayed, sometimes very different, at times I see it right away, and other times it takes me longer to "hear".

Heavenly Father, My tough circumstances can cause me to miss so many things You're teaching me. I know that it's hard to hear sometimes through my pain and grief. Lord, help me every day to close my eyes and just use my ears to hear. Help me to hear what You're teaching me, help me to hear You pour out Your love, Your Word, and Your healing on me. Help me to hear Your plan for me even in the midst of our pain. Draw me near to you, Lord, and guide me through each step of the way on this widow journey. In Your precious name, Amen.

July 7
Tears in a Bottle
By Kathleen Beard

Put my tears into Your bottle; Are they not in Your book?
Psalm 56:8b NKJV

I remember when I had my first baby.

Once the labor intensified, I thought to myself, "Ok, I want to go home now; I don't want to do this anymore." Well, of course, reality hit, and I knew I was in it for the long haul--like it or not.

I want John back. Can I just say?

In the months after he moved to Heaven, I heard myself saying the same thing, "Ok, I don't want to do this anymore, I'm ready for this movie to be over so we can go home and begin living normal again."

July 26 will mark five years since he moved to Heaven, and I miss him. This time of year John would be getting ready to end the school year, and we would be planning our summer. John had summer off, and that is when we had the most fun—we camped, or spent a few weeks traveling up Highway 1 in California or just hung around our little mountain town, sitting outside at the yogurt parlor downtown just people-watching. Every day with John was an adventure. I have photo albums stuffed with the same pictures, taken over and over each year—we didn't care if we had dozens of the same photos, we simply enjoyed the ride.

So, you can see why this time of year brings up all of those wonderful memories and why I just miss him so much.

John was a fairly new believer, while I was a little more seasoned in my faith. After years of praying for this very self-sufficient, self-confident man, he bowed humbly before Jesus and began devouring the Word of God until the dementia robbed his mind, will and emotions.

But it didn't rob his Spirit. During those four years of dementia, John grew to love the Word of God. I will never forget how God told me quietly one night, "The Spirit doesn't get dementia, Kathy." And it didn't.

In those first few, very raw months after he moved to Heaven, I hung on every word that would bring me comfort. Like a hungry orphan, I felt myself going from place to place asking for some Word to take away that awful abyss of pain. I wanted to know that the pain would have an end—that was so very important to me.

I wanted to skip over the process and move right into the healing.

Here is what Jesus did. He got my tears in His bottle and stored them up. He sent me widows who were fresh in their grief and every time this happened,

He opened up that bottle of my tears and let them spill into and mingle with the pain of another widow, and those tears were my healing and hers. Never underestimate the value of tears—Jesus doesn't. He stores them up to be used again and again.

Five years have passed. I still grieve—but it is not raw and it seems to be a scar rather than a wound. A wound still hurts when you press on it; a scar does not. The scar will always be there, but the wound has healed—*It has healed!*

Grief may be more acute in the Spring; that may always be with me and it's ok. But it isn't consuming me any longer, and if you are like me, you are desperate to know that there is life after death, not just for our loved ones, but for us here who are left to carry on. Jesus will redeem it all, He will not waste any of it and He holds our tears so that they can continue to heal both us, and others who grieve.

Oh thank You, Lord Jesus, for storing up my tears. Thank You for redeeming it all! I love You, Amen.

July 8
Weight of Glory
By Kathy Mills

For our present troubles are small and won't last very long. Yet they produce for us a glory that vastly outweighs them and will last forever! So we don't look at the troubles we can see now; rather, we fix our gaze on things that cannot be seen. For the things we see now will soon be gone, but the things we cannot see will last forever."

2 Corinthians 4:17-18 NLT

My life over the past four years without my husband has sometimes felt like I was in the middle of some strange emotional *tug of war* with myself! Some days I feel pulled by my memories of our past life together…recalling the moments I treasured and remembering all those tiny details that went into making our life together special. I'm suddenly wrestling with my desire to move forward with God beyond what my life held as Brad's wife. Today I gave in to just soaking in my past memories. After a little while (and a few tears too) I knew I needed to move on…but I hated the thought of letting go again of the plans Brad and I shared for the future that was never ours to have.

Sooo…feeling as though I had taken three steps forward in my "new life" and now suddenly feeling I just took two giant steps back…Jesus only allowed me to sit alone in my pity party of one for a brief while before sitting down beside me and helping me to recall some of the lessons I have been taught through His love these past years.

As difficult and painful as the process has been for me since Brad's death…I've learned through my loss to look inside my heart to find the things that had been keeping me from placing my complete trust and love in God.

Where I once had looked to Brad as my main source for a lifetime of love and security…it is in Jesus that I will always find the One true source that will always meet every (tangible and intangible) need my life yearns for. I discovered that God alone remains faithful in providing me with His abundant provisions of love and security for every day and every need.

In fact...through studying His Word and in prayer, the Lord has given me eyes to see beyond my own needs and even gives me glimpses of this world through His eyes so that I may know His heart more fully and respond to the needs of others with love and compassion. Although I still have those days and nights that I long for what I once had with Brad I know that there will be a day when the weight of this world will be replaced with the glorious weight of Heaven!

I just have to share this one experience with you...

After Brad died...and for months afterwards...I cried out many times to God that Brad's long days & hours of dying were too painful...the memory and thoughts I held of my precious husband being so tormented were more than I could bear. I wanted to "trust" God with how Brad died...but I struggled beyond imagine with the "why" it had to be "this way." Brad loved Jesus wholeheartedly...everyone who knew Brad, knew he had a heart for Christ. *"Why Lord would you allow him to suffer so greatly in death?"*

And then one morning as I laid in bed awake...once again crying for comfort from these tormenting thoughts... God blessed me with the most beautiful answer I would never have imagined seeing and hearing with my heart.

I saw myself walking along side of Jesus with my head turned towards Him as I spoke with him. (I was very animated while talking and moving my hands like I do when I am excited about something...yikes!). As we walked, Jesus' eyes were always on my face and He was smiling and even laughing at something I had said. (That image alone is "off the charts" wonderful...); Then Jesus suddenly stopped walking and turned his head looking straight ahead. So...of course I stopped too and turned my head to see what he was looking at.

As I looked ahead of us, I saw the back of a tall slender man wearing a white shirt with a head full of thick brown hair...and as he turned around to face us it was my most handsome and youthful husband Brad! Before even a moment went by...Brad cried out, "You're here!" He ran to me and scooped me up into his arms and swung me around and around saying over and over again, "You're here, you're here!"

As Brad swung me around I began to cry and thru my sobs I said..."I'm so sorry Brad, so sorry...you had to die in so much pain. I'm sorry..." Brad quickly stopped spinning me and as he closely held my face to his in the palms of his hands...with those beautiful deep set eyes fixed on my tear filled eyes, he said, "Oh Kathy...it was nothing...it is nothing!" While saying this his face broke out in the biggest smile...his face was filled with joy! I understood immediately what he meant...

You see...no matter the trials and heartache this life will bring...the moment...the very moment we exhale our last breath in this life and inhale our first breath of Heaven...all the pains and all the heartaches, every trial and troubles are washed away into the glory and beauty of our Lord's presence and our eternal home in Heaven!

What a gift...what amazing love God poured over my grieving heart on that morning. Finally... I found the peace I had been looking for and needed concerning Brad's last days and hours. I no longer ask God "Why?" or cry out to God asking him to "explain." I still shed some tears in missing Brad and I still don't know "why?" But...that question of "why?" no longer holds my attention or torments my heart. For I have a better answer than a reason could provide…It is to the joy of what is coming…the promise of one day I will be in heaven worshiping my Savior. One day, I will actually be walking along side of Jesus and we will be talking and laughing together. I will again be with Brad.

The promised *weight of glory* lifts off my heart all the *weight of pain* this world can ever give.

*For our present troubles are small and won't last very long. Yet they produce for us a glory that **vastly outweighs** them and will last forever*

July 9
A Single Mom's Grace-filled Saga
By Katie Oldham

Even youths will become weak and tired,
and young men will fall in exhaustion.
But those who trust in the LORD will find new strength.
They will soar high on wings like eagles.
They will run and not grow weary.
They will walk and not faint.
Isaiah 40: 30-31 NLT

The funeral was over. My family went home. The dust settled enough for me to evaluate my new environment. I looked at my two little girls and, wide-eyed, they stared back at me. I recall a strange surge of adrenaline and strong sense of motherhood that overtook me.

I was ready to take single parenting on with a calm confidence. I felt a closeness to God that reassured me, 'Everything is going to be just fine….right?'

The three of us would buck up, buckle in and 'be all that we could be'!

That adrenaline carried me for those first few months. I just stayed with my sweet girls as though our lives were suspended in time. Perhaps I noticed the world moving faster than life within my walls, but I turned a blind eye as friends and acquaintances moved on with their lives.

I kept mothering on my mind. Breakfast. The park. Puzzles. Preschool. Lunch. Dinner. Bath. Bedtime. Rewind...replay.....

Time raced on, and I felt the fog lifting. A growing sense of reality gnawed at my belly. I pushed it back. The beach. Play dates. Sweeping. Diapers. Groceries…Stand tall….remain steadfast…

Finally, frustration stuck its stinky foot in my door. I began bowing out of the activities requiring extra energy. That's all I needed, right God? Just lower my mothering standards, knowing He will water my wilting efforts.

That worked... for a while!

Until………everything felt like it was falling apart. There I was, sitting on the couch, staring at the fireplace and listening to two toddlers taking turns calling for me from bed. The air conditioner needed repair. Laundry piled up. My business suffered as I got pulled in every other direction.

Finally, it was more than I could handle emotionally, and while my love never lacked for my little girls, and my care was not neglectful, inside, I withdrew.

Grief set in.

Friends assured me that all I needed was time to suffer and space to grieve.

And as I grieved I began identifying with my title, 'widow. Over time, I embraced it. And as that grief stricken wife, I latched onto God's Word with disbelief still in my heart. What loss my children had endured! Them? Fatherless?!

I cried out of guilt knowing my girls were missing the best of me. As he lay ill, I told Kevin I wouldn't be the mom I was meant to be without him; I was afraid and wanted the praise he so often proudly paid me. How could I be the mom I wanted to be without his encouragement? My heart ached for the tangible touch and loving leadership of my other half.

But Kevin was gone. And so was the adrenaline. Parenting lacked its luster. The joy had been sucked out of it along with Kevin's death.

But my babies were my bliss! Didn't they deserve better? I had no choice.

God, grant me the grace to nurture my girls with enthusiastic desire. I did before! Fill my cup and fill the voids for something is missing!

Yes, Kevin was missing. But so was God!

I surrendered and drew close to God, craving His word upon waking each morning. It was HIM I was missing in motherhood. God was knocking at my door, drawing me near, but I had stayed too busy to notice.

As I listened to His Word, I felt His comforting embrace more and more each day.

I finally felt it: a new kind of contentment. It felt different than it had with Kevin as a co-parent. But, my passion for parenting returned.

I'm learning how to parent with grace, even within the walls of grief. His unconditional love for me leads me to the foot of the cross giving me the guidance I need. I again see the simple joys in childhood messiness. I feel even greater gratitude for my girls now!

I am blessed with the precious opportunity to parent my girls. And, no, I am not alone. HE makes me strong in my weakness.

July 10
Sunshine and Rain
By Teri Cox

Even in laughter the heart may ache, and joy may end in grief.
Proverbs 14:13 NIV

This is something from my journal written soon after my husband went home to be with Jesus.

*Two weeks ago tomorrow, my world changed forever. There is simply no other way to explain what happens when the hand of God comes to take away your greatest love on Earth. It is a forever change. I know in my head that God's love is a forever love and eternity is everything compared to the small part that we play in His plan here on Earth. Daryl and I had a purpose and it was based on our belief that Kingdom Work makes an eternal difference. **Daryl was not a common man** and we did not have a common marriage by today's standard. We **_LOVED_** each other with a love that is so rare and so precious* *many people spend their lives looking for it never to find it. We respected each other and were proud for and of one another. We each knew every single day how God had blessed us with this gift and we earnestly treasured it. We prayed together every morning before leaving for our day's journey. Daryl often thanked God for me by saying, "thank you for my beautiful wife and the treasure she is to me, protect our marriage."* **What an amazing thing to hear often over the past eleven years.**

I had a chance to reflect back on these words and memories, as I prepared to speak at a marriage conference last weekend. It is now some sixteen plus months since Daryl has been gone. The road has been more difficult than I can say, but you already know that, you are walking your own grief path where there are days that take your breath away and days that offer you bits or pieces of hope.

I have begun to find pieces of Teri along this path. Pieces of who I was, before there was a Teri and Daryl, are returning ever so slowly. What I find fascinating though is how they have changed. I do not have the same perspectives anymore because I understand what it is to be married to a man who loved me as Christ loved the church. I am forever changed because of a life well lived.

My prayer for each of us it that someday our children, families, friends, churches, and communities will be able to speak the same of us; that they are forever changed by our lives being well lived. God still has a plan and purpose for each one of us. His scenes for us are not complete. He loves us as much today as He ever has. Do not give up, do not give in, press on and lean into Him. His arms are wide open.

Keep me as the apple of your eye;
hide me in the shadow of your wings.
Psalm 17:8 NIV

July 11
One Widow's Psalm
By Linda Lint

I cry out to God Most High,
to God who will fulfill His purpose for me.
Psalm 57:2 NIV

In the early days I cried – a lot.

Some days I carried a box of tissues with me around the house, and I never left home without an ample supply – I knew I would need them.

To say that "I cried out to God" is really an understatement – it was really more like wailing – a deep, deep down cry that would not be silenced. I had so many questions – there was so much I did not understand. I was prepared for my beloved to pass; however, as I have told many people, I was in no way at all prepared for life "after" -life "after" that phone call at 3:36 am with two simple words that changed the landscape of my life forever – "he's passed". Simple words, direct, gently said by the kind nurse – but they screamed at me and catapulted me into a place of aloneness like I have never experienced before. I was alone, truly alone. I just didn't know what to do with myself or where to turn next. What was I supposed to do with my life now. What was my purpose? My children were grown and my husband was gone.........

Of course, I "knew" God loved me.

Of course, I "knew" He would never forsake me.

Of course, I "knew" He was "there" but w.h.e.r.e.?

Turning away from the anger and despair, I decided instead to press in and seek Him with my entire being and all of my energy. I turned to His Word and read and read and read. But – I could find no comfort in the familiar stories from the Old Testament and the wondrous miracles and happenings in the Gospels and the Acts of the Apostles.

Then I re- discovered the Psalms – I mean I r.e.a.l.l.y re-discovered the Psalms. Here was something to which I could relate. Here was David in the depths of despair and loneliness crying out to His God and being honest with Him about the way he felt – even with a "hint" of frustration at times.

I realized then that I needed to be "honest" with God and tell Him how it really was with me. That's when I wrote this – my Psalm to the Lord:

Lord, where are you?
I hate this loneliness. I fear I will soon be consumed by it for I can feel it draining the life from me, drying me out and leaving me dreary and barren.
Your beauty is around me at twilight with the gentle glow of pink from the sunset. Yet, the tears in my eyes blur its presence.
When, Lord, will this end? How long will I be able to endure this emptiness? What purpose is this serving – as I weep over my loss?

There is no question "why", for I understand You are sovereign.

You have made heaven and earth and have declared the number of each man's days.

You know when each rose blooms and when it will fade.

You have set the time of the sun's rising and setting.

Your hand rests upon all of creation.

Trees sway in the wind that You send.

Crops grow in the rain You provide.

The morning sky is painted with Your fingers, the same fingers that knit me together in the secret place of my mother's womb.

Yet, I ponder on all of these mighty works of Yours and still my heart is aching — aching for his hello, aching for his gentle touch, aching for his smile, aching to be home with You — for he is there with you.

I cannot understand — yet I have hope:

Hope as I recall Your mighty deeds of the past.

Hope that rests in the promise of Your Word that says You have a plan and a purpose for me and that those who mourn shall be comforted and that there are new mercies for each day.

Hope that causes me to declare, even through these tears: YOU ALONE ARE GOD. There is none other than You.

And through the tears and the pain I am learning that You are indeed enough and Your grace is sufficient.

I took the risk — and found that being "honest" with God was just exactly what I needed to do. This journey is by far the hardest one of my life. However, it is a journey into my "purpose". He has a plan for me and each day He meets me where I am and gently guides me along the path.

Dear one, in your pain and sorrow dare to be honest with Him — He loves you so — He wants to hear it all — He does not want you to carry it like a heavy burden upon your back. Give it to Him – He stands ready to lift it from you. I promise – but more importantly – HE promises.

July 12
The Yet-Praise
By Liz Anne Wright

> *Why, my soul, are you downcast?*
> *Why so disturbed within me?*
> *Put your hope in God,*
> *for I will yet praise him,*
> *my Savior and my God.*
>
> *Psalm 42:11 NIV*

Quite a few years ago, we knew a woman who would quote this verse when bad things happened. My group of friends and I then invented what we called yet-praises.

We read this verse to mean that in any and all circumstances you can praise God…even if you don't feel like it, even if you don't see the situation as a good thing, even if the world seems to be crashing down around you.

We started calling each other not with prayer concerns but with yet-praises.

And we had quite a few of them. At that time, this friend was adopting a young teen from the Philippines. Because of weird circumstances and more complications than I could name (she could write a book), the process took *over four years*. It was hard, but we tried to look at each set-back as a yet-praise as I journeyed with her in prayer through that time. When her sweet daughter finally arrived in the States, I bawled like a baby.

But isn't that what the Bible calls us to do…to count it *all* joy? I love the way The Message says these verses in James:

Consider it a sheer gift, friends, when tests and challenges come at you from all sides. You know that under pressure, your faith-life is forced into the open and shows its true colors. So don't try to get out of anything prematurely. Let it do its work so you become mature and well-developed, not deficient in any way. James 1:2-9

This process is not easy, sisters. I am well aware of that. Six years into this journey, and I often feel like Israel in the desert…purposeless and punished, spinning my wheels instead of living a joy-filled life.

But that is when I need to return to the yet-praise…right there in the midst of the trials and the stresses…right there when I need God to work the most…and am able to see His hand the least. He is in control, He is sovereign, He does hold me in the palm of His hand. Just because my view is dim, doesn't mean He isn't working.

I need only to go to the scriptures to see that…over and over again.

God's people praised Him in captivity and during persecution…much more difficult circumstances than my worst widow days. How can I not praise Him?

David messed up badly, having another man killed and taking his wife, yet he could go to his

Father and restore that relationship, praise God for who He is and what He had done for David, even after his son died. How can I not praise Him?

Yet, I need to make the *conscious effort* to turn my trials, large and small, into praises.

I faced several this week—prayer concerns that become praises because of God's involvement and obvious love for me expressed daily, weekly, sometimes hourly.

Here they are, and what I could find in them to praise God for:

• The toilet broke *again* – *yet I can praise Him* because my sweet friend Michelle sent her husband to fix it…again.

• We never got the mulch on the yard this summer – *yet I can praise Him* because a friend with a landscaping company is sending his guys over to spread the mulch *and* get the yard ready for winter.

• I have trouble keeping the house clean, or even neat, or even passable – *yet I can praise Him* because I have a nice, warm home to live in safely and comfortably with my children.

• I have a messy car, covered with sticky stuff from too many snacks eaten in it – *yet I can praise Him* because I have a working car, and a friend who is a mechanic who keeps it that way.

• We miss Keith every hour of every day, even six years later – *yet I can praise Him* because of the life Keith lived, which still mightily affects us today…and for his sons who grow to be more like their dad each day.

• I sat alone in worship Sunday morning – *yet I can praise Him* as my oldest played on stage in the worship band...honoring God with his playing and his honest worship.

I ask you, sisters, to look at your own trials. It really, really stinks to be a widow. It is hard work to walk around with half of yourself on the other side of Heaven. *Yet we can praise God* for who He is and what He has done.

After all, some day, when our time here is done...we get to enjoy that same reward. God has sent His one and only Son to die in our place so we can go to Him as our husbands have done...to live in perfect peace and comfort in eternity...with our Lord.

And that is something to praise God to the highest Heavens for!

Dear Father, help me to look at my trials as praises. Help me to see them as light and momentary, as You do. Help me to have the strength to face them, to lean on You when the going gets tough and I feel like giving up. Help to walk forward, knowing that someday this widow walk will be over and I will stand before Your glorious throne. Help me to live each day like I believe that. And forgive me for the days that I have trouble seeing the blessing. Help me to see it. In Jesus' name, Amen.

July 13
Yet Praise Continued
By Liz Anne Wright

Are there times from your life recently that you can do like Liz Anne did, and write Yet Praise after them?

• The _____ needs repairing, Yet will I praise…

• I miss my husband, Yet will I praise…

• My friends don't understand my grief, Yet will I praise…

• Another loss came quickly on the heels of the loss of my spouse, Yet will I praise…

• I miss the love of a spouse, Yet will I praise…

Take a few minutes to write these Yet Praises out on a paper that you can post on your bathroom mirror or somewhere you will be reminded often or even in your journal.

Or write out this verse on a post-it and stick to your dash board.

Why, my soul, are you downcast?
Why so disturbed within me?
Put your hope in God,
for I will yet praise him,
my Savior and my God.

Psalm 42:11

July 14
Morning By Morning...
By Kit Hinkle

Because of the Lord's great love we are not consumed,
for his compassions never fail.
They are new every morning;
great is your faithfulness.
Lamentations 3:22-23 NIV

Did you wake this morning with that pit in your stomach? Let's erase it! Start fresh, renewed by His mercies, sister!

Let's begin the day with a prayer just for you:
Dear Father of All Who Need Your Peace on this Morning,

Reach Your strong hand down to each of us ladies who awake this beautiful morning to the thoughts that stream in.

- To the thoughts of the day and all she has on her plate--give her

But seek first his kingdom and his righteousness, and all these things will be given to you as well. Matthew 6:33 NIV

- To the thoughts of her children and how will they grow up healthy and normal without an earthly father to guide them--give her

A father to the fatherless, a defender of widows, is God in his holy dwelling. Psalm 68:5 NIV

- To her thoughts about strained friendships and hurts that she carries over a judgment another person laid upon her.

115

Do not take advantage of the widow or the fatherless. If you do and they cry out to me, I will certainly hear their cry. My anger will be aroused...Exodus 22:22-24 NIV

• To the same thoughts about offenses others have made against her.

Be kind and compassionate to one another, forgiving each other, just as in Christ God forgave you. Ephesians 4:32 NIV

• To the thoughts of finances, and where the security of her future lies.

So do not worry, saying, 'What shall we eat?' or 'What shall we drink?' or 'What shall we wear?' For the pagans run after all these things, and your heavenly Father knows that you need them. 33 But seek first his kingdom and his righteousness, and all these things will be given to you as well. Matthew 6:31-33NIV

• To worries over her health, and that next appointment with her doctor.

For our light and momentary troubles are achieving for us an eternal glory that far outweighs them all. 2 Corinthians 4:17NIV

• For an overall anxiety, for which she recognizes a twisting in her soul coming from some core dilemma she cannot seem to place a finger on.

For I know the plans I have for you," declares the Lord, "plans to prosper you and not to harm you, plans to give you hope and a future. Jeremiah 29:11NIV

Father, let Your sun rise on me today, reminding me that Your Son rose on that day--just for me. Give me conviction in my heart that You love me specifically, and that I am lifted as a shining star--chosen specifically by You. Amen

Shake off that sense that as a widow, there is some kind of reproach on you, sister. The Lord gets that some of us feel that way, and He wants you to remember that reproach no more!

Do not be afraid; you will not be put to shame.
Do not fear disgrace; you will not be humiliated.
You will forget the shame of your youth
and remember no more the reproach of your widowhood.
Isaiah 54:4 NIV

If you haven't been moved yet, try hearing God's word sung so beautifully in the hymn, <u>Great Is Thy Faithfulness.</u> Let the words swirl around in your head all day.

July 15
The Bride
By Sarah Rodriguez

Not long after losing my husband, I sat down on my bed and began to think about the things I was missing the most. This is what I found--I was missing the deep trust between the two of us, being protected, cared for, and loved. I loved being a wife. I missed being a wife. I missed being HIS wife. I missed my groom. I loved everything that goes along with a Christian marriage the commitment, the comfort of knowing he belonged to me. I missed being his bride. As I thought through these things I felt God whisper in my heart, softly saying, "You are my bride. I am your groom." At first, I nearly dismissed the thought as typical things we hear in church about being "the bride of Christ". It was one of those statements I have heard so many times it might have lost its impact. I tried to push those words away, but they wouldn't leave me: "You are my bride."

For the next few days that proclamation stuck around in my heart, not budging. Then I began to break it down:

- I missed having deep trust.

But I trust in Your unfailing love;
my heart rejoices in Your salvation.
Psalm 13:5

- I missed being protected.

How I love You, Lord! You are my defender. The Lord is my protector; He is my strong fortress. My God is my protection, and with Him I am safe. He protects me like a shield; He defends me and keeps me safe.
Psalm 18:1

- I missed being cared for.

The Lord watches over you—
the Lord is your shade at your right hand.
Psalm 121:5

- I missed being loved.

Your love, O LORD, reaches to the heavens,
Your faithfulness to the skies.
Psalm 36:5

The more I dug into the truth of God's word, the more I realized that what He was gently whispering to me was true. I am His bride. Everything I was missing in my husband I can truly find in Him. Does that mean I don't miss my true groom on this earth? Absolutely not. I miss him with every fiber of my being. But the truth is, there is not one need my spouse provided that Jesus cannot meet. There is not one characteristic I loved about my husband that God does not possess. And the greatest truth? As much as my husband loved me, no one loves me more than Jesus. Jesus love is perfect. It is without spot or blemish. It is a love He gave His life for and He did it just for me. Each day I look to Jesus to meet me where I am and fill every empty space.

I look to Him to speak to me gently and lavish His love on me. There can be no greater romance. Me as His bride, He as my groom. Jesus, the lover of my soul. I am His and He is mine.

July 16
A New Year, a New Chapter
By Nancy Howell

I did it.

Well, let me rephrase that. *We* did it.

In a whirlwind trip, my boys and I traveled to Kansas, where my late husband is buried. We haven't been there since Thanksgiving. This trip was significant because we were going to be there on the observation of his first year of being in Heaven. I don't like to call it the first anniversary of his death. Anniversaries are typically happy events, marked with parties, flowers, cards, and laughter.

My younger son, now nine, had not yet visited his dad's grave. His grief had been different from his brother's—he avoided feeling anything for months, but is now working through many grief issues. I hoped that both boys would want to visit the grave, but don't push it. Who am I to tell them how to feel, how to process the loss of the most important male in their lives? We're on this journey together, in it for the long haul, but we are all at various stages. When we're on the same wavelength we cry, reminisce, and laugh together. When we're not, we pull together, helping each other out.

We compiled a list of accomplishments that we've made during this first year, so we could share them with Mark at his earthly body's resting place. It's a long one, with items as varied as one son's beginning piano lessons to another's selection to the Little League All Star team to both of them being elected student council representatives at school. My successes ranged from taking over his outdoors column for our local newspaper to figuring out how to ride a lawn mower to attending She Speaks conference the past month. We've come together as a team. Above all else, we've asked God to keep holding our hands.

I trekked alone to his grave to read the list. The drought had left the grass brown and prickly so I ended up sitting on top of his ground-level mausoleum. I felt like I was sitting on his lap, as I'd done countless times in the past twenty-five years. As I began to read, the narration became a one-sided animated conversation. I added in extra commentary as necessary—laughing, crying, and smiling throughout. He is there. Not just his earthly body, but in his glorious heavenly body. It is palpable, so much so I feel I can reach out and touch him.

As I left the cemetery, I spotted a large bird flying overhead. It was a bald eagle, the first I had seen in central Kansas—ever. It swooped over me, landing in a tall tree nearby. It followed me in my truck, flying from tree to tree, settling in not fifty feet from the driveway. I got a better look before he flew away. Wow! What a gift God gave me in sighting that majestic bird.

The scripture running through my head, over and over, is:

> *He gives strength to those who are tired and more power to those who are weak.*
> *Even children become tired and need to rest, and young people trip and fall.*
> *But the people who trust the Lord will become strong again.*
> *They will rise up as an eagle in the sky; they will run and not need rest; they will walk and not become tired.*
> *Isaiah 40: 29-31 NCV*

Both boys accompanied me to their daddy's graveside our last night in Kansas. We all three sat on the top of the mausoleum as a full moon began to rise. Each boy individually knelt at that grave and copious tears flowed. Each of them conversed with their heavenly Father and their earthly daddy for a long time. I gave them the space and privacy to grieve. As I stood only a few feet away, I fought to keep from scooping them up in my arms. I so wanted to take their grief away.

Then I felt God whispering, "Let them feel this. Don't worry—I have them in My arms."

We've made it through the first year of grief. Although it was hard to see at the time, as I look back, I see God's hand in everything. He was part of every decision, every blessing, every day. His presence is real, tangible, and solid. He stands ready to scoop us up when we are in pain or unable to walk another step. He is actively working to weave something beautiful for my family of three as we move forward with our lives.

We are becoming strong again.

Dear friends, God will never abandon you.

He will never forsake you.

And in the darkest hours of your grief, whenever you aren't sure if you can even take a breath,

He is there.

Open your hands and your heart. Although your life will never be the same as it was, it will be good again.

God will make sure of it.

Dear heavenly Father, I pray for Your blessing today. Bless my loved ones, too. Enlarge my territories so I can comfort those who need me and be an example to those who think there is no future awaiting them. Please keep Your hand on me, and keep me from evil. Let me not cause pain, instead let me trust in You, and You alone. Give me the strength to rise up like the majestic eagles, and walk forward on my journey without tiring. I will give You all the praise and the glory, for You make my life worth living. In Your son Jesus' name I pray, Amen.

July 17
No Need For Gadgets
By Liz Anne Wright

Even though I walk through the darkest valley,
I will fear no evil, for you are with me;
your rod and your staff, they comfort me.

Psalm 23:4 NIV

I got a new bread maker for Christmas. My old one had literally fallen apart, and my sweet sister bought me a new one. I am so excited! Not only is bread from the bread maker healthier, it also makes the house smell *wonderful.*

But, I must admit that part of what I like best is the *convenience.* Put in the ingredients, push a button, and *walk away.* The machine does all the work.

We are blessed to have all the modern conveniences we do in our households today. Washer and dryer, fridge and freezer, make our lives so much easier than our forefathers. We can accomplish tasks on the run instead of over the course of a day, squeezing in the next load of laundry or dishes as we run to all the activities, fun and necessary, which are in our lives.

I think sometimes, though, we are tempted to treat our grief this same way. We try to rush through the difficult moments, find ways to conveniently deal with the sadness and pain that are a natural part of this journey. We try to find a way around the *hard work* that grief is at times, looking for an easier way. We have pressure from those around us to "move on," "get over it," "start again" from well-meaning friends and family.

But grief is not like that. It is not a linear journey, one with an ultimate destination. It is a progression, and progress cannot always be made in the same way the world sees progress.

I have taken a lot of cues on how to grieve, and gotten a lot of comfort from, the Psalms, but particularly in Psalm 23...particularly in verse 4.

Even though I walk through the valley of the shadow of death...

The Psalmist does not indicate that he hurries through his grief, trying to get quickly, conveniently to the other side. He *walks*. And, as he walks, *God is with him*. If he were hurrying, he might outrun God's plan for the moment. He might not fully or completely heal in areas that are needed before moving on to the next portion of his life. By walking, he takes the time needed to be comfortable with what has happened.

The Psalmist keeps walking...walking forward, walking with God, walking the path laid before him...not avoiding it, not getting stuck in the middle, not turning back, not using anything fancy. He walks *through* the valley of the shadow of death, not jumping over the pain and sorrow, not trying to shorten the journey by hurrying.

I imagine him much like me, slogging through some moments, almost too weary to go on, but knowing it is necessary, part of the plan...and ultimately...for my good. Again, focusing on the fact that God is *with* him...with *me*.

And, down the road, he achieves a place of comfort, a place where he has come to, if not an understanding, at least a peace about what has happened in his life. How long did this take? Only he and God know.

So, sweet sisters, as we contemplate all our modern conveniences, may we not get caught up into the trap of trying to make our grief convenient...convenient for us or for anyone else. It is what it is...God-allowed, though we may not understand the reason.

May we focus on doing it the way He wants us to, walking with our hand in His, no matter how long it takes.

May we keep moving forward, not stuck in the valley, but, trusting in Him, walking the steps slowly as we need to, *crawling* when we need to, but always moving forward in our grief.

And may we always, *always* be holding the hand of the Author and Perfecter of our faith as we continue on the journey through this valley.

May God bless you on your journey!

Heavenly Father, grief is hard. I want to grieve well and completely, Lord, in the way that You want me to, learning what I need to but not getting stuck somewhere in the valley. Help me to lean on You to grieve, first and foremost. Help me to not get caught up in looking for convenience in our grief, but to balance that with continuing to move forward on the path You have already seen. Hold my hand when I cry, when I stumble, when I fall. I are so thankful You are here with me, every step of the way. In Your precious Son's name I pray, Amen.

July 18
The Gospel of His Grace
By Sheryl Pepple

However, I consider my life worth nothing to me, if only I may finish the race and complete the task the Lord Jesus has given me-the task of testifying to the gospel of God's grace.
                                      Acts 20:24NIV 1984

It sneaks up on you; the recognition that once again God is showing His tender love for you. My dear sisters, this journey is so difficult, please allow me to encourage you today by sharing a sweet story of how God has shown His personal love and grace to me during this journey.

When my oldest daughter Jen married in 2009, my husband and I were elated because we had dreamed of the day we would get to share the joy of being grandparents with little ones running around. When my husband was killed in September 2011, that dream died with him. Being a grandparent with my husband was a very precious dream to me because my first marriage had ended in divorce when my daughters were just 5 and 2 years old. God's plan was different than mine, but He knew and cared about the desires of my heart.

On May 13, 2012, eight months after my husband's death, we celebrated my first Mother's Day without my sweet husband. Both of my daughters came into town to spend the weekend with me. As we were having breakfast that morning, I awkwardly tried to lighten the mood by teasing my oldest daughter; "I would have thought you would have tried to make it a great Mother's Day by telling me you're pregnant". We all laughed and headed off to church. During the church service my daughter started feeling nauseous and began doing some math in her head. On the way home from church she stopped and bought a pregnancy test and then quickly came to show me the results. None of us could believe it! How truly special for all of us to find out on that Mother's Day that we would soon have a new little one to love and cherish! But the story of God's grace doesn't end there...

One day, during my daughter's pregnancy, I was looking for some paperwork to deal with some of the legal issues that arose from my husband's death. I had given up trying to find it and then finally decided to look in one last place – the cabinet beside his bed, which I had not been in since his death.

When I opened his cabinet, there to my amazement was a Texas A&M onesie, size 6-12 months. Both of my daughters went to Texas A&M and as the saying goes- they bleed maroon. They are avid fans, to say the least! So how is it that my husband bought a Texas A&M onesie (that fit perfectly during football season this year) two years before it was needed? My husband was notorious for being a last minute shopper. How did I find it at just the right time? All I can attribute it to is God's grace! God knew the desire of my heart to share being a grandparent with my husband. He knew the absolute joy I would receive by seeing my precious grandson Riley in the onesie *his grandpa bought him*! God also knew it would bring me great joy to testify to the gospel of His Grace and for that I am most grateful!

Let us complete the race set before us- all the while testifying about His Grace!

Dear heavenly Father, You are such a loving God! Thank You for being with us each step of the way. Thank You for showering us with Your Grace and love, many times when we least expect it. Please watch over me today, please comfort me and encourage me in a mighty way! Help me, Father, to complete the race, testifying about Your Grace, for Your Glory! In Your Son's Holy and Precious name, Amen.

<u>July 19</u>
It's All Good!
By Sherry Rickard

> *The Lord is close to the brokenhearted*
> *and saves those who are crushed in spirit.*
> *Psalm 34:18 NIV*

My husband passed away in 2011.

He had been battling a rare blood cancer for over four years. In 2010, it became apparent that the only chance to save his life would be to undergo a bone marrow transplant. After much prayer, tremendous love from our family and friends, and a divine certainty that we were in God's will, we took a leave of absence from our jobs and left Northern Virginia for Duke Hospital in Durham, North Carolina.

My husband, Bill, received his transplant on January 14, 2011. Bill was forty-two and strong in body and spirit. The first few days were fine, however as we waited for the engrafting to occur, Bill began to contract infections (viral, fungal, bacterial, etc.) because he had no immune system. He also contracted graft versus host disease in his skin and G.I. tract—a major cause of death among transplant victims.

As we watched Christina Aguilera sing the National Anthem in the 2011 Super Bowl, I turned to comment on her mistake and Bill was unresponsive. A team rushed in and he was whisked away to ICU. I called our family, and they started making plans to come from various areas of the country. I will never forget the last words that Bill spoke to me a few days before he passed away. He said, "I love you always my beautiful wife!" Bill fought for several days more.

For a whole day, the word "Goodbye" kept whispering in my head and heart. I knew it was the Lord and that He was lovingly preparing me for His answer to my prayers, but I kept pushing it away and hiding from it. Finally, the next morning, I couldn't sleep and woke up early and prayed. God told me that Bill's testimony had to be told but that Bill would not be the one to tell it; I would. He then lovingly reminded me that I had to say goodbye...not forever, but for now.

As I made my way to the hospital with Bill's wedding band and his favorite blanket, I realized that I had to tell Bill it was OK to go. I entered the ICU and I pulled back his sheet and covered him gently with his favorite soft blanket and slipped his wedding band on his finger. I gently laid my head on the pillow beside his ear and whispered, "I don't want you to go, but if Jesus comes for you, go ahead, I'll be OK. I love you!" He opened and closed his eyes several times and made eye contact with me.

As eighteen members of our family gathered around his bedside in the ICU, we sang hymns and took turns kissing and hugging him and he looked each one of us in the eyes and blinked goodbye to each of us. I know the moment our Savior showed up and took my sweet Bill by the hand and led him over into Gloryland. His countenance became that of a little boy full of wonder and his beautiful lips formed a perfect "O" as though he was already singing praises to the Lord.

Later, we made our way back to the hotel and as I sat in the lobby surrounded by family, the front desk found me and handed me a beautiful flower arrangement. I thought friends had sent it - after all it was Valentine's Day. I opened the card and it said, "I love you always, my beautiful wife. Love, Bill"

God didn't leave me in that room in the ICU. He didn't leave me in that hotel lobby crying over the last Valentine's flowers I would receive from my husband. He gave me hope. I will see my husband again. I have a Savior that cares about my every thought and need. He seeks my company all day and never fails me.

Three years down the road, I have discovered I would not have picked this journey if given the choice, but I like who I have become because of what has happened to me. God's not done with me yet and I'm excited to see the plans He has for my life and future.

My husband loved the Lord and, on a day all about love, he went Home to be with his Love. That is hopeful! Today, on this day that celebrates love, may you think about the Lord who loves you—and will never leave you, no matter what. That's a promise from Him.

Dear Lord, Thank You for allowing me to love and be loved. Thank You for assurance that I have an eternal home in Heaven with You when my earthly ministry is finished. Thank You for Valentine's Day and a new understanding of love that I have because of You. Amen

July 20
Man-Cubs Dating...And Other Monsters
By Liz Anne Wright

> *Point your kids in the right direction—*
> *when they're old they won't be lost.*
> Proverbs 22:6 *The Message*

My oldest son, Alex, is now fourteen. He is over six feet tall, and has a man voice. And sometimes I am scared to death.

Parenting a *boy* alone is tricky business for this momma. I grew up with a sister. I don't know the drill with raising boys...much less raising *four* boys. I expected to have Keith here to help me with this.

God had other plans.

I'm not complaining, really...just trying to figure out how to do this without a man in the house. Any of you there with me?

I don't know if raising one gender over another is any easier...each, I'm sure, has its challenges. I just long to do the best job I can turning these young men under my charge into the best men of God they can be...to the glory of their father...and their Father.

The latest challenge is in the area of...gulp...girls and dating.

Keith and I had talked a bit about how we were going to handle the dating times for our boys...but just a bit. After all, Alex was not quite nine when his dad died. We figured we had time.

To our way of thinking, there were two main ways to approach the boy-girl relationships at the high school level: dating and courtship. Dating, what we had both been through, to us, involved more exploration and social involvement with a person of the opposite sex, without any serious intent or expectation…a focus on there being multiple people whom you would spend time with, none of whom you may have considered as a possible marriage partner. On the other hand, our view of courtship was that it was intended for the purpose of finding a spouse…thus increasing the seriousness of each potential "girlfriend" and the relationship with her…and with her family.

We had discussed both dating and courtship as possibilities. We knew families who had been successful with both methods in keeping their kids pure and in line with God's will. I was leaning to courtship; Keith was undecided.

Now, without Keith and his wise input, I have to determine how to handle things in this arena.

Scary stuff.

It's tough out there for kids today, as I am sure you all know. So many temptations any time you turn on the TV…or walk down the street…or pick up a book or magazine! So much freedom that can so easily be abused! So many opportunities for long-lasting physical and emotional consequences!

I was not, am not, perfect…and I long for my boys to have an easier time navigating the waters of dating and finding a mate than I did.

So, how do I approach this, when I don't think anything remotely like a boy…don't even understand the male gender?

For starters, after prayerful consideration, I have determined that we will take an approach to dating that is more courtship-based. Alex and I have discussed my reasons for this, and he is on board with my decision. Well, maybe not totally *fine*, but he is yielding to my authority in this matter, and understands where I am coming from.

Just another one of those firsts without his dad here for guidance. And it stinks.

How do you know when to snuggle them and when to tell them to "man up?" How do you know when you have given them enough information and when you have really given them more than they need…or want…to know?

I am *blessed beyond measure* that there are Godly men in Alex's life who are willing and able to give me advice. I know I can call them any time, any day…and Alex knows that he can, too.

But…I still wish I had Keith's take on the situation…and its solution.

When Keith was still alive, I would send the boys to their rooms when I needed to think about what to do with them in discipline situations. Often, I would call their dad to vent…and ask for his wise input.

Not long after Keith died, I told the boys that whenever they were in trouble and needed disciplining, they should expect to spend more time in time-out in their rooms. This was because now my conversations with Dad would take a little longer (prayer to the Father as opposed to a phone call to Keith at work on the tough situations).

That's how I am handling these man-cub choices as well: prayerful consideration…and time.

Whenever I make snap decisions, I tend to over-react. Mostly, I need to rest in the Lord and prayerfully consider all that is happening with my growing boys.

I need to lean in and lean on the Lord. He loves my kids more than I do. He knows their needs…and my needs…more than I do.

He actually has more invested than I do…the blood of His Son.

Ultimately, we will traverse these waters of puberty, dating, and marriage…and all the other waters…through God's grace and by His strength.

If we let Him work, He will. He has…He will again. That's what He promises.

And I need to trust my son as well. He has a good head on his shoulders. Praise God, he is a lot like his dad.

Alex's last comment on the subject was this: "You know, Mom, I have heard it put this way: treat every girl like you would want a guy to treat your daughter."

Wise advice!

I am praising God for this young man and the joy of raising him, even if it is without his dad.

We'll be alright. By God's grace, I know we will.

Father, I thank You, first and foremost, for being my wise counsel in any and all situations. I pray that You give me a heart of confidence and trust in You to realize that I can raise our sons to be men of God. Alone, I can do nothing, but through You I can have victory in this area…and I praise You for that. In Jesus' name. Amen.

July 21
All Things Together
By Sarah Rodriguez

When you pass through the waters, I will be with you;
and when you pass through the rivers, they will not sweep over
you. When you walk through the fire, you will not be burned;
the flames will not set you ablaze.

Isaiah 43:2 NIV

Recently I have been talking to my circle of friends about my grief and my sadness over losing my husband. It is all encompassing. I think about my husband Joel much of the day. I cry every single day- numerous times a day. I know there is a grief process and it'll be one that I will probably spend years walking through. I have mentally prepared myself for this to be an extremely long process of difficult moments mixed with small victories. When you spend a decade of your life with someone, then lose them in an instant, very few people can understand how painful it is unless you've been there. It is the deepest pain I have ever felt, the darkest place I have ever been to.

But.

And there is a "but".

There is hope deep within me in the midst of my circumstance.

In 1 Thessalonians it talks about not grieving as ones who have no hope. I will not grieve as one who has no hope. It's important to note it and it's important for me to proclaim it. I know where my husband is and he is with Jesus. I know he is happy and he is whole. I know he is walking in the fullness of everything that God has ever had for him. I know I will see him again and once I do it will seem like the time apart was the blink of an eye. I also know God has promised He has not left me or my son. He has promised He will take care of my family. He has promised He will restore what was stolen from me. And His biggest promise? That He will turn my ashes into a thing of beauty like only He can do.

I know there have been many people who read my personal blog who stopped reading the day my husband passed away. To them the story of our family is over. Know this-the story of our family is just beginning. My husband's story is just beginning. Yes, his journey on this earth has physically ended but the impact of his life has not and will not end. God will turn the pain of losing him into a testimony of His greatness because that is what He promises to do.

And we know that in all things God works for the good of those who love him, who have been called according to his purpose. Romans 8:28 NIV

Our best days as a family are yet to be. I know that statement may be hard to understand because of what we have lost. But it comes from our deep belief in our God and His ability to restore what was lost and work all things together for our good. I don't look at anything with Joel's life as an end point. He's not here physically but he still lives and we will see him again. Until then my son and I are on a mission to tell his story and for God to still get His glory. We know he will be cheering us on every step of the way.

I had a friend get in touch with me and what he said touched me beyond words. He told me about a dream he had about my husband in Heaven and he was looking down on Milo and I and he started to be sad for all of the pain we were walking through. But then Jesus went to Joel and was whispering in his ear and Joel was filled with joy once again. He said it was as if Jesus was showing him all of the things God had in store for our family and it filled my husband with so much joy because he almost could not believe all of the incredible plans God had for us. We know our goodbye to Joel was not the end. And until we are reunited with him we have some work to do and we will make sure he is at the center of it. I've said before God has never failed us and He won't start now and even in the midst of my grief I believe that now more than ever before. We grieve-with hope.

Dear God-I cling to your truth that no matter how it feels, You have never left or forsaken me. I thank You that I can hold on tight to that hope in the midst of my pain. I thank You that You are turning the ashes of my life into beauty and that even now You are working all things together for my good. Amen

July 22
Clogged
By Danita Hiles

*You will go out in **joy** and be led forth in peace;*
the mountains and hills will burst into song before you,
and all the trees of the field will clap their hands.
Isaiah 5512 NIV

My coffee maker stopped working this weekend. For this coffee lover (translation: addict) this was a dreadful turn of events. Time on the phone with the company folks revealed the problem. Water wasn't getting pulled from the reservoir because the channel was clogged. The machine turned on and hummed and whirled but at the end, nothing. Nada. Not one drip of lovely coffee poured into my cup. The solution apparently is de-scaling: running a vinegar solution through to get rid of the hard-water yuk that had built up.

Now here is where it got personal. 'You're clogged', God whispered. 'Just like your coffee maker, you are clogged with some yuk.'

Sure, I had been making all the right noises and going through the motions of being a Jesus girl, trusting God and living my faith, but there was a coating of discontentment that had settled on my heart. And maybe even the tiniest root of bitterness. Ouch.

This clogging business doesn't happen overnight. Not in my coffee maker. And not in me. Clogs slowly build up over time.

Those questioning whispers of ~ 'why this?', and 'what about me?' and 'what if?' Clog.

That undercurrent of resentment toward someone else's 'normal'? Clog

Simmering impatience with…oh just about everyone? Clog.

Worrying out loud and calling it prayer? Choosing pouting over praise? Clog. Clog. Ugly clog.

My pastor hit the nail on the head during his sermon yesterday. (Don't you love it when God is dealing with you on something and makes sure you get it by repetition ?)

Here, Paul is writing to the churches in Corinthians about some churches in Macedonia:

2 Corinthians 8:2 NIV   Out of the most severe trial, their overflowing joy and their extreme poverty welled up in rich generosity.

These folks in Macedonia were not living a perfect easy life. They were going through some stuff. For Paul to call it a severe trial, it has to have been something notable. Yet, they were able to overflow with joy and generosity to others in spite of what they were personally experiencing.

How was this possible? Just go up a verse. Verse 1 - "...we want you to know about the grace God has given the Macedonian churches. '   They were only able to overflow because of God's grace which flowed through them. Wow.

I have not been feeling very grace-full lately. You can't give what you don't have. You can't pour out, what isn't flowing through you. It is not about how perfect our life is (or isn't). Stuff is going to happen in life. Hard stuff. Ugly stuff. Stuff we would much rather didn't'. Severe trial sounds about right. But even so, we_can still overflow with joy. Because of His grace.

Lord, today give me a vinegar rinse to clean out all of the clogs of comparison and discontentment and worry and resentment. And then, Lord, bring on the grace Let it flow, let it flow. As I get my mind off of me and my 'stuff' and onto You, may I raise my tear-stained face and empty coffee cup to the sky and be simply drenched in Your grace. Grace that spills out in overflowing joy on everyone I meet. Amen

P.S. Thank you, Lord, for coffee

July 23
Thank Those Who Know To Just Listen
By Kit Hinkle

The Lord is a stronghold for the oppressed,
a stronghold in times of trouble.

Psalm 9:9 ESV

When you really need comfort, don't you appreciate those loved ones who get that they need say nothing but to just be with you and understand?

I have to admit, I had to ignore a lot of comments that could have added more salt to my wound of loss and just consider the sweet intention that was meant by the words. Well-meaning people want to find the right words for your situation, but sometimes, the words that work best are simply no words, but a comforting way of just being with you. Have you had to overlook some faux pas?

I recall reading Lisa Beamer's book, <u>Let's Roll,</u> about her husband Todd who died courageously foiling the terrorists' plans to possibly crash a jetliner into our nation's White House.

As she sat in her dark bedroom the night of Todd's death, in deep pain, avoiding the many words of many well-meaning friends, one sweet believing Christian friend sat by her side and said absolutely nothing. Just quietly kept watch and prayed as Lisa let the reality of her loss settle over her.

Do you have a friend who will do this for you? If so, let her know what a sweet salve she is to you.

And for those who have perhaps tried to help with the wrong words, forgive them, and try to love them for the intentions they had for healing words. Many in this world aren't equipped with the righteousness given by our Lord Jesus Christ and try with only the world's tools at hand, to help in situations that call for far more spiritual tools.

Blessings, sisters, in loving on our sisters and brothers as they try their best to help in times of loss.

July 24
Forty Years of Heartache
By Leah Stirewalt

> *Though the fig tree does not bud*
> *and there are no grapes on the vines,*
> *though the olive crop fails*
> *and the fields produce no food,*
> *though there are no sheep in the pen*
> *and no cattle in the stalls,*
> ***YET** I will rejoice in the LORD,*
> *I will be joyful in God my Savior.*
> *Habakkuk 3:17-18 NIV*

In preparation for the lesson I was about to teach from the Old Testament book of Ruth, I posed the following question to my ladies Sunday School class: "As a child or youth, what was one of the greatest heartaches you've ever experienced that, in hindsight, might not have been that tragic of a heartache in the grand scheme of life?" You know the kind…those we experience as children that appear as if our world will fall apart at any moment as a result of this newly discovered sorrow. I made it clear that I wasn't talking about those heartaches that had lasting effects: divorce of parents, death in the family, abuse, etc. I simply wanted to hear about those that most of us now can look back upon and laugh.

For me, I shared about the time I was in first grade and humiliated by my teacher. To set the stage, I was a rule-follower all the way. I was known as the "teacher's pet", because I made good grades, kept my mouth shut when I was asked to, and never disobeyed an instruction given to the class. This particular morning, I had to make a quick trip to the bathroom. Upon returning to my seat, I picked up my pencil to await the words we would soon hear from Mrs. Sizemore, "Now begin your worksheet, class." To my dismay, Mrs. Sizemore walked right up to me, and asked me to hold out my hand, which she proceeded to smack with a ruler, and then said, "I told you not to pick up your pencil until I said so!"

I was shocked and humiliated. The tears started to pour. I couldn't even utter words to defend myself. I later learned that she apparently instructed the class not to pick up our pencils until she gave the command to do so. Because I was in the bathroom, I missed that announcement. I never even tried to defend myself. I took the punishment and never forgot about that day the rest of my first grade year.

My heart still hurts a little to remember that 6-year-old girl – wet with tears – all because of an innocent misunderstanding. But, I can also laugh at that one a bit too, knowing now that was one of many heartaches (some much larger and some still small) set to come my way over the next few decades:

- The destroying of my glass figurines by an angry sibling
- The separation and divorce of my parents
- A disastrous move to FL at the end of my 8th grade year
- Two unfortunate remarriages and divorces by my mother
- My high school sweetheart unexpectedly breaking up with me after 18 months of dating
- My pants splitting straight down the back seam while I was standing in the very front of the church one Sunday evening
- Painful surgeries
- Infertility
- Weight management battles

And…this is just the tip of the iceberg. I've had forty years of heartaches, but nothing compares to the sorrow I experienced on May 4, 2011 when my precious husband took his own life. In retrospect…

- That slap on the hand in 1st grade was laughable
- My broken, treasured figurines could be replaced
- I ended up moving back to NC from FL making that move not so miserable after all
- God protected my mother and siblings from those unfortunate marriages
- My high school sweetheart wasn't all he was cracked up to be anyway
- My split pants…well, let's just say that's one I'd simply like to forget about
- I healed from my surgeries
- I was blessed to be able to give birth to one child – even with minor fertility treatment

• And the weight management battles – well, they wage on – but, that too will be over one day

However, the tragedy of my husband's death...the sorrow in becoming a widow...the despair and loneliness in losing my helpmate and best friend...I don't ever expect to look back on this time and think "Aww...that wasn't so bad after all." I will never discount this horrific and painful time as being anything less than what it's been.

However...yes, there's a however...

The bigger tragedy? You might be asking how I can even imagine a bigger tragedy. Honestly, the most distressful heartache I can imagine is not meeting my Savior face-to-face in Heaven one day. Does that make these dark days easier? Sometimes yes and sometimes no. Regardless, the day I enter His arms, He will wipe away every tear and all sorrow will vanquish, and this lifetime of heartache will be completely erased.

For now, I rely on His Holy Spirit to carry me through the most excruciating pain I've ever felt, trusting that He will do just as He promised. And...when that blessed day comes...this recent heartache will end up in the list with all the others.

July 25
Love Letter
By Danita Hiles

My dear daughter,
Yes, I am here. Even when you don't feel me. Even when you don't see me at work, I am right

there. My strong hand rests in the small of your back, gently urging you forward.

My tender eyes gaze into yours even as you stare into the impossibility of your future.

This has been a difficult season, I know. I have been there for every question, through every tear and each cry of desperation. I am with you. I go before you.

Don't ever doubt that.

I have seen you at church, offering me all that you have. Whether a voice raised in praise or a hand clenched to stifle tears, I see your sacrifice and it is beautiful to me.

I am there at your dining table, as you try to recreate normal for your family during a simple family dinner. Know that I am there in the empty chair, gazing at you with eyes of love.

And on birthdays and holidays and school performance days, when the remembering is yet a little harder, know that I am especially close. I hear your cry of 'it's not fair'. I know, precious daughter, I know.

Know that I am at work, making something beautiful. The dark spaces in the tapestry of your life simply serve to reflect the light of who I am. Many will be drawn to you because they see me in your life. And see that, in spite of it all, you still believe. There is much that will not be understood this side of heaven. Stand on the promises in my word. They are the only sure foundation for your ever shifting emotions.

I love you. I love you. I love you.

Your heavenly Father

Let the beloved of the LORD rest secure in him,
for he shields him all day long,
and the one the LORD loves rests between his shoulders.
Deuteronomy 33:12 NIV

July 26
The Empty Chair
By Karen Emberlin

Fear not, for I am with you. Do not be dismayed.
I am your God.
I will strengthen you; I will help you;
I will uphold you with my victorious right hand.
Isaiah 41:10 TLB

Have you been faced with an "empty chair" beside you?

During the past nineteen months there have been many times I have experienced the empty chair syndrome. For quite some time it seemed almost everywhere I would go, the empty chair was there too! Meal times, church services, family gatherings, and just a relaxing evening at home were all reminders that I was alone.

I thought I was doing much better until a few days ago when the empty chair appeared in another "first" situation. In a ten day period I faced two surgical procedures, the first ones since the loss of my husband. In the past few years, I have experienced some tough medical issues, but my husband was always sitting in the chair beside me as we talked with doctors, went through tests and tried to make the best decisions for my care. He was always at my bedside helping in any way he could to reassure me and make me comfortable. I knew he would always be there when I woke up, making sure I was cared for in the best possible way.

This time as I checked in for surgery, the empty chair brought back so many memories! It seemed to represent the pain and emptiness that wanted to consume me. Please understand, I am so thankful for a wonderful circle of family and friends who cared about me, prayed for me, and made sure I was not alone, but it just was not the same. No one could take the place of my husband!

While waiting in a small quiet room prior to surgery, I stared at the empty chair remembering what it used to be like when my husband was there to hold my hand and reassure me. As I prayed and focused on verses from His Word, I realized that instead of my husband, God was sitting in the empty chair, loving, listening, and waiting for me to hear Him.

Was I still concerned – certainly! Did I still miss my husband – I sure did! However, I knew God was sitting there with me providing a peace that passes all understanding.

The loss of my husband leaves an empty chair but God is sitting there waiting for me to spend time with Him. The relationship my husband and I enjoyed happened because we spent time together and shared our joys and sorrows with each other. God wants me to talk to Him and share my feelings just like I did with my husband. He also wants me to be still and listen to what He has to say to me. Sometimes it is hard to talk to an "unseen body" – I would feel much more comfortable talking to someone I could see and touch. However, He promises that He will be with us always. **In faith I can see Jesus in the empty chair!**

Lord, help me begin each day believing You are all I need to continue this journey of widowhood. May I accept Your plan knowing that You have allowed this pain and loss in our lives. Help me take the pain and hurt to a chair that is never empty and allow healing in Your time. May I discover the purpose You have for me. Amen

July 27
Chosen
By Rene Zonner

> *...the Lord has chosen you to be his treasured possession*
> *Deuteronomy 14:2 NIV*

Do you know what I miss most about my husband? I miss hugs for no reason—catching his eye across a crowded room and knowing exactly what he is thinking. I miss the inside jokes we shared and "that" look from him. I miss knowing out of all the people on this planet, he chose me to spend the rest of his life with, and it was me he came home to everyday. I miss feeling special, set apart...

I miss being chosen.

For the sixteen years before my husband John died suddenly of a heart attack in August 2010, I had something I really craved. Someone here, in the flesh, who had chosen me above all others. I took great comfort in this fact and being a wife was very important to me. Until he died, I never realized just how important being chosen was to me.

Truth is, most of my self-worth and identity came from knowing I was enough for someone, a physical flesh and blood person. My feeling of security depended on John choosing me daily. And now that I'm single again, not having this daily affirmation for almost three years now has brought my insecurities to the surface.

Oh sure, my parents love me but they have to, right?. They didn't choose me—I was just given to them. My three young children love me (OK, some days more than others) but again, they didn't ask to be my children, so what choice did they have? My friends choose to love me, but the reality is I am lower on the totem pole than their own spouses and families.

So who chooses me?

Having grown up in the church, I know the answer to that intellectually—God. But when I became a widow, this fact did not provide the comfort it probably should have. God loved me enough to take care of me and my children. He promised He would redeem my future, and He would use the loss to my good and to glorify Him. After all, He has provided for me in countless ways both materially and spiritually, stamping His fingerprint on my life throughout this season of widowhood

So why wasn't He enough for me? What was missing? Why did I feel unloved and unwanted?

Only recently did I get an inkling to why.

See, when I heard "God loves the world", all I could think was "great, He loves everyone just the same" and "I'm nothing special, just another face in the crowd".

And that is not what I desire. I want to be special! I want to be chosen! John's gone, and now, because of my circumstances, I just wasn't feeling special. I was allowing my circumstances to tell me I wasn't chosen.

But, those were my feelings—not Truth.

I am chosen! In Deuteronomy 14:2 God tells me I am His own special treasure. Isaiah 41:3 exclaims I am precious to God. Psalm 139:17-18 shouts God thinks of me all the time. Isaiah 49:16 reminds me God has engraved my name on His hand. Rene Zonner is engraved on the same hand that made the stars!

He's speaking to me!

But not just to me! These verses are for you as well. God is not limited to human constraints of only being able to do or think of one or even a few things at a time. He can love each of us as like there is no one else to love. He can think of me all the time and still think of you all the time. I am not just some face in the crowd, and neither are you. Psalm 139:13 tells us God knit us together in our mother's womb. He knows you and me intimately. He knows us better than our husbands ever could, and he still chooses us. I know this is hard to grasp for some of you, and I am still trying to wrap my brain around it myself. But we must hold onto this truth about God. It is vital that we find our security, our value and our self-worth in the God who loves us personally.

Let's not depend on others to provide what only God can.

Heavenly Father, I pray that I understand the personal and intimate love You have for me. Help me to see that even though my loved one is not here to make me feel special, it's okay because I am treasured by the God of the universe. I ask You to make real to me just how wide and deep Your love is. I pray to know that I am truly chosen. Amen

July 28
A Widow's Walk Is Never Carved In Stone
By Kit Hinkle

Through these he has given us his very great and precious promises, so that through them you may participate in the divine nature and escape the corruption in the world caused by evil desires.

2 Peter 1:4 NIV

Sometimes thriving in life as a widow means listening to how God wants you to participate in His divine nature. It's different for each of us because a widow's walk is never carved in stone. The Lord asks some of us to weather it quietly—grieving and accepting the loss as your heart allows you to—one step at a time. The Lord sometimes asks us to move forward boldly, letting go of fear so that through our boldness, we protect the younger ones He has put in our care from the corruption in the world.

When the Lord leads you to step forward boldly, you might have fear over what the world thinks of you as you as you move forward and lead your own life into the future without leaning on an earthly husband. I think of the widow, Ruth, and her obedience to the Lord and how it led to bold steps on her part, choosing to remain with her mother-in-law, choosing to gather grain behind the harvesters in

Boaz's fields, and presenting herself to Boaz in a humble but brazen gesture to petition him to claim her as his wife.

Ruth was brave, and yet so loved by the Lord for her obedience that He blessed her by allowing the bloodline of His only Son to run through her.

Imagine how fear could grip a woman in her situation faced with deciding whom to align herself with, how to provide for herself, and whether to pursue a new marriage. As a widow, you might feel it too. Widowhood can be a life full of fear if you allow yourself to get overwhelmed.

I'm reminded today to stop fear in its tracks for it is not from the Lord. I consider what my pastor told me after he took three of my sons on a Gettysburg Father-son retreat. He reassured me that decisions I've made since Tom has died have been good ones, evidenced by a Christ awareness my kids displayed on that trip with him. He told me my children seem to have no trouble going against the grain of the world. In other words, under my leadership which came straight from the guidance of the Lord, for the time being, they have escaped "*the corruption in the world caused by evil desires*".

The Lord sometimes speaks through the words of blessings from others, and my pastor's words were well-timed at a moment when I felt overwhelmed. I marvel at their progress, because many times my decisions go against the grain of this world, to the point of coming under scrutiny of others who aren't sure what to think when a widow steps out in boldness. Some don't understand that my choices are not my own. I've allowed the Lord to lead.

Sometimes people of the world want to tell you how as a widow you've been beaten. You've suffered loss. You're supposed to recoil, curl up in a ball and feel sorry for yourself.

There is that place where you need to be alone and recover. And sometimes that can take a while, but there was a point after Tom died where the Lord told me, grieve but don't recoil. Break free. Burst forth in radiance because my four boys will watch and follow. They will be marked forever in their souls by the choices I make as a widow.

They will either see themselves as victims or see themselves as stepping forward by following and staying safely inside the Eye of the storm—accepting that what Satan doles out with the intention of evil, God takes and turns around for His Glory.

If you feel a prompting in your heart to follow a purpose the Lord has laid out for you, I encourage you to pray about it. Don't let fear stop you. Let the peace that only comes from the Holy Spirit prevail over you. He will lead you. It's His *great and precious promise.*

July 29
The Grief Hawk
By Erika Graham

> *Therefore my dear brothers and sisters, stand firm.*
> *Let nothing move you.*
> *Always give yourselves fully to the work of the Lord,*
> *because you know that your labor in the Lord*
> *is not in vain.*
>
> *I Corinthians 15:58 NIV*

A hawk might eat my dog! That's what I was told at our last vet visit. Seriously, I was told a hawk might swoop down and grab my dog. This is quite comical to my friends and family, who've been on this rather funny and a bit nutty puppy journey with me.

You see, I love to do special things to commemorate the significant days of my husband's life, most importantly his earth birthday and heaven birthday (the day he went home). I've done different interesting things that include; attending a Yankee game on his b-day, competing in a five mile mud run on the 2nd year anniversary of his passing, and most recently, buying an eight week old puppy.

This fall, out to lunch with a friend on what would have been my husband's 39th earth birthday, I planned to stop next door to "window" shop at a puppy store. With little intention of purchasing a dog, I walked out with our little Ellie Belle, a Lhasa Poo (Lassa Apsa and Poodle mix). Ellie has brought so much joy and fun to our home. She is a blessing I did not anticipate.

But, she is a puppy! My philosophy was a little dog would only create a little mess, and while that is true, that little mess is ALL over my house ALL the time. I had no clue little dogs take so long to potty train, and are so much more delicate than a big dog. Plus, she is long haired, so a few vet visits ago I was advised that she should be brushed at least two to three times a day to prevent matting. Say what?

At this visit, as the vet was warning me about the danger of large predatory birds taking my Ellie Belle, I really didn't know whether to laugh or cry. I envisioned that scene from "The Proposal" where

Sandra Bullock's character is running around tempting the hawk with the little dog trying to convince him to release her cell phone, except I'd be running around waving my phone at the hawk trying to get him to release my Ellie.

Over the last several months, this puppy has been so much work and has brought added stress. Yet, she's also brought us fun and happiness. It's been an adventure and a welcomed distraction, and I know that my labor will create a wonderful family pet.

As I was filling the kids in on the perils of a large bird attack, I started to think how this little puppy journey has mirrored my widow journey. Although puppy woes, compared to grief, are trivial, short-lived, and in my case full of funny stories, here's what I realized; I had absolutely no anticipation of becoming a widow. I went into it knowing nothing about true grief. I often felt at any moment I was going to get carried off by the grief "hawk". I had "messes" all over the place some days. I needed to be loved or "brushed" often by my friends and family, especially in those early days, and this grief journey has many stages with their own *unique to me* time frame.

My puppy is getting better with every passing day, and the great news is God IS growing and changing me too. I won't always be in today's stage. I will not be carried away by that grief hawk and my messy days are becoming fewer and farther between. Now I can love on others who are in the trenches of the early days of grief. He is drawing me nearer to Him and making my faith stronger. I can see clearly that in Him my labor through grief and willingness to allow Him to guide me is NOT in vain.

Sisters, God's word is clear, if we give ourselves fully to Him in this grief "work", then through Him it will not be in vain. He will heal us, protect us, guide us, and even reward us. I pray today that you can see and feel how God is working through your grief labor in many big and small ways.

And if you need a good distraction, you need to get an Ellie Belle! . ;)

July 30
Four Years
By Rene Zonner

> *But do not forget this one thing dear friends:*
> *With the Lord a day is like a thousand years*
> *and a thousand years are like a day.*
> *The Lord is not slow in keeping his promises*
> *as some understand slowness…*
> *2 Peter 3:8-9 NIV*

This August will be four years since I became a widow.

Really? Four years?

Some days it seems like just yesterday John died…most days, it feels like a lifetime ago.

In so many ways, life has gotten easier. The children and I have found our groove. We have learned the new normal. The heavy grief we felt in the early days is past. Life has moved on and it's good.

But, if I am completely honest, it's still hard in some ways. Many times I feel worn down by the reality of being the only adult in a family with three children. There are days whenever everyone needs to be at a different place all at the same time. Yard work and home maintenance get neglected because there is just not enough time in the day. I need to provide for my family financially so I have to make time to work on my business. Laundry and dishes pile up more than I would like. Discipline gets a bit lax at times because I am just too tired to stand my ground. Doctor appointments, haircuts, meal planning…all fall on my shoulders.

And then there is the biggest challenge of all, being the spiritual leader of the family. Most days I feel like I should be and could be doing more in this area. I believe, as the woman, I was designed to be the helpmate in this area, not the head. But here I am, the reluctant head of the household. The children's spiritual life is in my hands and I feel I am at a disadvantage. I have to admit, I get discouraged.

When things started to settle down after John's death, I prayed and asked God if this was it for me. I wanted to know if I was ever going to be loved again. I believe with my whole heart I heard God whisper to me that I would have the strong, Christian marriage I desired if I just remembered to do things His way. I still believe it, but you know what? I didn't really think I would still be waiting almost four years later. I persevered through the tough times clinging to the belief that this was only temporary. God never gave me a time frame though. It was me who just assumed it would happen sooner rather than later.

I couldn't imagine God would allow my boys to be on the verge of the critical teenage years without a strong male influence. I didn't believe my sweet baby girl would get to the point of asking why all of her friends had daddies but she didn't. I never dreamed I would go without being held lovingly by a man for almost four years. I've endured dating disappointments, single parenting, and loneliness with the hope that before too long, I would see God's promise fulfilled. But I'm still waiting.

On good days, I trust God and believe His timing is perfect and that a new love hasn't happened for a good reason. On those good days, I am satisfied with God as my husband. But then there are those days when I doubt. I doubt I truly heard God's promise, I doubt He even wants to fulfill the promise, and I doubt I'm good enough to deserve the promise. It's those times when I find it hard to be satisfied with God alone. Those are the days I feel as if God has forgotten me.

Feelings aren't truth, however. The truth is God does keep His promises and wants to fulfill them (1 Thessalonians 5:24). The truth is I can do this widow, single mom thing with God's help (Philippians 4:13). The truth is I am loved by God (John 3:16) and by the many wonderful people God has brought into my life. The truth is God is enough if I allow Him to be.

Widowhood, single parenting, these were not part of God's ultimate design for us, but we live in a fallen world and I've learned it's okay to be discouraged and frustrated at times. You may have heard the promise of a new marriage, or maybe you've heard the promise of a new life purpose, or a special God dream. You may also be wondering when these things will happen. You may feel the frustration and disappointment when it doesn't happen as quickly as you thought. The key is to not stay there. When the feelings come, let them run their course.

Pretending you're fine will not make it better. Get into the Bible and let God's truth wash over you and renew your hope.

God's timing is always perfect. I'm still learning to trust his timing. To trust He sees the big picture while I can only see the speck right in front of me. To trust He has my best interest at heart. Come, dear sisters, and learn to trust with me.

Father, I pray that I will be strengthened and encouraged by the knowledge that Your timing is perfect. I believe You have a plan for me. Holy Spirit, remind me, when I am discouraged, of the truth of God's love for me. Thank You for Your patience with me when I question Your will for my lives. Thank You that I am not forgotten. Amen

July 31
The Eternal Victory
By Sarah Rodriguez

*When the perishable puts on the imperishable,
and the mortal puts on immortality,
then shall come to pass the saying that is written:
Death is swallowed up in victory.
1 Corinthians 15:54 NIV*

What happens when you don't receive the answer you wanted to a prayer? I've been thinking lately about what constitutes a victory when we pray and believe for something. When I prayed for my husband to live and he didn't, did that mean my prayers failed? I struggled for a really long time with the answer to that question. Initially my honest answer would be, yes they did fail. That's wholeheartedly how it felt. I was confused for so long at how I could believe so completely for God's promises and they didn't come to pass. If you would ask me if it felt like we obtained a victory in our prayers I would have answered no.

I lost my husband and best friend and have to live the rest of my life without him. My son lost his father. I have to raise a child alone. I have to live life as a "widow," a term I despise. I have to learn to live without my best friend and greatest companion. No part of that sounds like I was victorious in my prayers.

But then I think of my husband Joel and how the answer of our prayers looks from his perspective. He is totally and completely healed. He is no longer stuck in his failing and mortal body. He is no longer sick. He is with Jesus and has never felt more alive. He is no longer struggling or in pain. He knows God and His ways with the greatest of intimacy. His story was a light in the darkness to literally thousands of people around the world, and continues to be. The only downside I can see to where he is, is those he loves are not with him. But to him it is only a little while until we join him, so that downside disappears.

The more I thought about it, the more I understood God did not ignore my prayers. We were victorious in what we asked of Him. God gave us a victory. He just took what many see as an earthly victory and instead gave Joel the eternal victory.

We long to keep our mortal bodies chugging forward as long as they can. We long to keep our loved ones here with us. We long for more time on this earth. We long for more worldly experiences in a world that is broken, full of sickness, pain and disappointments. We long to be in a place that is truly not our home. We long for "time" that is fleeting, instead of a destiny that is eternal. We are missing it. We are longing for the wrong things. We should really long for a Heaven where death has been defeated and tears are no more. In that place there is life to the fullest. In that place sickness is defeated. In that place death is overcome. In that place life truly begins, not here. There. Yet we long for this world. We believe true victory is staying here just a little bit longer. When that doesn't happen we concede defeat when in reality we should be proclaiming victory.

The token question is always "how could a loving God allow something like this to happen?" The only answer I believe is because He saw a greater purpose in the end result. He saw greater purpose for me. He saw greater purpose for Joel. He saw greater purpose for our family. He saw greater purpose for Joel's story. We haven't quite seen it or understood it yet but one day we will.

One day He will make everything known and everything new.

It has changed the way I view the answer to the prayers for my husband. God answered me when I called. He bestowed not upon us a tragedy but a triumph…a triumph given to us by the One who understands a victory more than anyone else: He who conquered death and gave it to us eternally.

Dear God, I thank You that I have victory through Your son, Jesus. I thank You that I walk in that victory every day. Amen

August

<u>August 1</u>
The Thorn of Widowhood
By Nancy Howell

Because of the extravagance of those revelations, and so I wouldn't get a big head, I was given the gift of a handicap to keep me in constant touch with my limitations.

Satan's angel did his best to get me down; what he in fact did was push me to my knees.

No danger then of walking around high and mighty! At first I didn't think of it as a gift, and begged God to remove it. Three times I did that, and then he told me,

My grace is enough; it's all you need.

My strength comes into its own in your weakness.

Once I heard that, I was glad to let it happen. I quit focusing on the handicap and began appreciating the gift. It was a case of Christ's strength moving in on my weakness.

Now I take limitations in stride, and with good cheer, these limitations that cut me down to size--abuse, accidents, opposition, bad breaks.

I just let Christ take over! And so the weaker I get, the stronger I become.

2 Corinthians 12:7-10 MSG

The Apostle Paul wrote the above words to the church in Corinth. Other translations of the text use "physical limitation" or "thorn" instead of handicap.

Thorn is the word I like best.

What was Paul's thorn?

Did he have a physical impairment--bad eyesight, epilepsy, a limp?

Or was his thorn spiritual in nature?

As my two-year mark as a widow approached this week, the above verses kept coming to me, over and over and over. Now I'm certainly no Biblical scholar, but I am familiar with Paul's story, of asking God to take his "thorn" away, three times.

We all have thorns. Not one of us is "thorn-free." The thorn of widowhood pierced my flesh on July 30, 2011. I wasn't ready for it. None of us are. It's something we all have in common.

We come from different places geographically. We are of different denominations and faiths. We may be financially secure or we may be struggling. We might have young children at home, or be an empty nester, or childless. Our skin color, our hair color, and our ages most likely run the spectrum. Politically we might not see eye to eye.

But we all bear the same thorn. And that thorn binds us together.

Who hasn't asked God to remove this thorn?
I have asked many times. On the day it was evident
that, short of a miracle, I would become a widow, I
begged, pleaded, cried, and tried to bargain with God.
"God, please take this! You have to heal him. You
cannot take this daddy away from his two little boys!"

But it happened. A few minutes before
midnight on that fateful day, I became a member of
this club that no one ever wants to join.

So, what do you do with a thorn of this
magnitude? It's overwhelming at times.

I look to Paul. He was human. He prayed for
God to take away his thorn. And God answered.

God doesn't always answer our prayers in the
way that we want. Instead of removing Paul's thorn,
He tells him "my grace is enough; it's all you need!"

God's grace is enough.

It's all that you need.

No matter the thorn, no matter how deep, no
matter how messy and infected it might get, God's
infinite grace is enough.

Two years ago, my future looked bleak to me.
I lost the love of my life, and was left a single mother
to two young boys. I didn't have a clue as to what I
would do, where I would live, how I would make it
without my husband. I told folks I felt as if my arms
had been cut off.

But God's grace was sufficient. He swept in,
picked up the pieces of my brokenness, and showed
me that although my life would be different, it could
still be beautiful and worth living.

"My strength comes into its own in your
weakness."

Those first few months, whenever the storm that was my life would threaten to drown me, I would whisper, "When I am weak, You are strong..."

Okay, I won't lie. Sometimes, alone in my car, tears welling up, overwhelmed by life in general, I would scream it, but only when my windows were rolled up. No one heard me but God. He was the only one that mattered.

After Paul was given the message of God's grace, I love what he did. He quit dwelling on the thorn, instead choosing to appreciate the gift.

"Widow" will be an identifying thorn in each of us for the rest of our earthly lives.

If we're stuck with it, why not choose to embrace it, and attempt to appreciate the gift?

I may never appreciate having this thorn, but I can appreciate how my life has re-formed around it.

Allow God's grace to fashion a new life around your thorn. Never ever forget what you had, but let God's strength come shining through your weakness.

It doesn't happen overnight. It doesn't happen quickly. But bit by bit, step by step, immersing yourself in God's words, praying for guidance and discernment, you will begin to heal.

God's grace is enough. It's all you need. Let Christ take over.

In your weakness, His strength becomes evident. In turn, you gain strength from Him.

Father, I come to You today bearing the thorns of widowhood. Remind me that no matter how long I've been in this club, I have Your grace and Your strength with me always. I pray that the friendships I'm making in this sisterhood will continue to grow. In Jesus' name I ask it all, Amen.

August 2
Serving, An Opportunity For Healing
By Sheryl Pepple

For I was hungry and you gave me something to eat, I was thirsty and you gave me something to drink, I was a stranger and you invited me in.
Matthew 25:35 NIV

Somewhere along the line you have probably heard the advice "it helps to get your mind off of yourself and focus on others" or something to that effect. This is something I have heard many times in my life. The first few days after my husband was killed by a drunk driver in September 2011 were busy as we handled all the arrangements for the memorial service and spent time with our friends and family; but as the crowd began to thin, I started thinking – what do I do now? It wasn't long before I remembered "it helps to get your mind off yourself and focus on others" and I quickly decided to jump into action.

About six weeks after my husband's death, our church was organizing a trip to downtown Dallas to serve the homeless. Before I even realized what I was doing, I signed up to serve. We gathered at the church at 6:00am that chilly fall morning and carpooled downtown to an outside church that ministers to the homeless in a parking lot. The moment I stepped out of the car, I was gripped with an overwhelming feeling that I had made a terrible mistake. Immediately I cried out in prayer, "God I don't know what to do, I have nothing left to give." God quickly brought to mind a book I had read years ago about the homeless. It talked about one of the struggles for homeless people is that they feel invisible. I thought, boy I can relate to that. I felt like I was screaming on the inside but nobody could really see me. About that time, God led me over to the food serving area and a still voice in my spirit said, "Look them in the eye and tell them you are happy to see them." Serving spoonful after spoonful of eggs, looking person after person in the eye, I repeated "Good morning, I am so happy to see you today". With each spoonful, and with each greeting, I felt the blessing of God's love and the joy of being used as a vessel for His presence. I was, and continue to be, grateful that He equips us to serve others. Over the last two years He has given me many opportunities to serve and I can look back and see what an integral part of the healing process it has been for me.

Soon I will be traveling to the Philippines for my third mission trip to that area since my husband's death. It is a mission field we used to serve in together. The first trip was incredibly difficult. Each time I go back, I am stronger. Each time, God has used serving as an opportunity to further my healing. Our last trip was in November. It was an exciting trip in many regards. To some it was exciting because yes, we were there for Typhoon Yolanda, the worst storm in world history, but even more exciting was the opportunity to go door to door with some of the local pastors sharing the gospel. In just ninety minutes we were privileged to see thirty-five people accept Christ as their personal Lord and Savior. No matter how difficult life gets, no matter how broken I feel, God continues to give me the opportunity and the strength to serve. And step by step – the healing continues.

Dear Heavenly Father, thank You for how You have fearfully and wonderfully made me. Thank You for the sacrifice of Your Son who died on the Cross that we might be reconciled to You, our Glorious Father. Thank You that You created me for a purpose and that You promise to equip me for that which You have called me to do. Father, I pray that You would continue to comfort and heal me on this journey. I pray that You would guide me according to Your will that I may fulfill the purpose for which You have uniquely created me. Thank You, Father, for loving me more than I can possibly imagine! In Your Son's Holy and Precious Name, Amen

August 3
Fear Not Tomorrow, God is Already There!!
By Karen Emberlin

> *For I am the Lord your God*
> *who takes hold of your right hand*
> *and says to you,*
> *Do not fear; I will help you.*
> Isaiah 41:13 NIV

Is today one of those intense grief days? Are you struggling with the fear of the unknowns in your life without your husband?

I remember clearly the feeling of fear gripping my entire being the morning I awoke realizing my husband was not in a "deep sleep" but had journeyed to his heavenly home. I could not imagine how I was ever going to face another tomorrow without him. For 48 years he was my constant companion, best friend, lover, father to our children, working partner, protector and so much more. We truly had become "one" and depended on each other all of the time. Many people said they rarely saw one of us without the other!

"Tomorrow" is a word often filled with promise and hope. With the challenges I faced, the thought of tomorrow left me feeling anxious, inadequate, and overpowered. I knew in order to conquer the fear of tomorrow I had to trust God to be my constant companion and my ultimate caretaker. I needed to focus on Him, who He is, His promises, and His plan for me.

The following words were written in one of the devotionals I use: *"I am with you continually, so don't be intimidated by fear. Though it stalks you, it cannot harm you, as long as you cling to My hand. Keep your eyes on Me, enjoying Peace in My Presence."*

Music has always touched my heart allowing me to communicate with God when I cannot focus as I should. A few weeks before my husband's passing we had the privilege of attending the first performance of "Fear Not Tomorrow – A Worship Experience" at our church. The music and the message it brought seemed so timely - we were facing uncertain tomorrows relating to our business. Little did I know how my tomorrows would change in just a short time – but God did – He was already there and preparing me through the ministry of this music.

I have spent many hours listening and absorbing the message of this music in the past few months. My husband fulfilled many roles and took care of me during the time I was allowed to spend with him. It is hard to imagine that anyone else would care that much for me - but God does! His love is never ending, His arms are there to hold and embrace me, and He's in control of every tomorrow I will face.

I'd like to share the words from one of the songs:

Come all who are broken
Come if you're afraid
Come taste His sweet water
Come feel His embrace
There's more than existing
There's more He will give
The future is waiting
This time is yours to live
His arms always open
They're aching to hold
The bounties of heaven
Are waiting to flow
Let go what restrains you
Let God fill your soul
You don't know tomorrow
But you know Who's in control
Fear not tomorrow
God is already there
Through your joy or in sorrow
Every moment is in His care
Let the song of His love
Sing over you and declare
Fear not tomorrow
God is already there *

My dear Sisters, I continually need to ask the Lord's help to face tomorrow, and what it might bring, without fear. In the midst of my heartache I forget and take my eyes off of Jesus. And that's whenever the fear creeps back in! I pray He will continue to remind each of us of His greatness and Love for us, and His presence in all of our tomorrows as we walk this unwanted Journey of Widowhood.

*Fear Not Tomorrow by:

Sarah Mentzer, Brandee Vandergriff, and Tim Paul

Used by Permission – Copyright © 2011 Risen Music Publishing

August 4
Remembering with Love, Tears, and Stones
By Nancy Howell

When life is heavy and hard to take, go off by yourself. Enter the silence. Bow in prayer. Don't ask questions: Wait for hope to appear. Don't run from trouble. Take it full-face. The "worst" is never the worst. Why? Because the Master won't ever walk out and fail to return. If he works severely, he also works tenderly. His stockpiles of loyal love are immense. He takes no pleasure in making life hard, in throwing roadblocks in the way....

Lamentations 3:28-33 The Message

The past two weeks of my life have been just that--heavy and hard to take. I travelled back to my late husband's home state, Kansas, where he is buried in his home church's country cemetery. Although

Texas has been home for over twenty years, Mark's heart and roots were always in rural McPherson county, Kansas.

His family has farmed land continuously there for over a hundred years. When he died unexpectedly, it was an easy decision to make, returning his earthly body to rest 1/4 mile from the land he loved so fervently. He's buried close to his father and various other relatives, including his great great-grandparents.

His ground-level mausoleum is beautifully simple. Its curves blend in with the landscape. His marker is succinct and to the point. Decorating it is a challenge, since flowers and other items slide from the top.

Since we live in Texas, six hours from his gravesite, my boys and I don't visit often. Last week, while boys were in church camp, I travelled north to take care of some business. Our sons asked me to visit Dad's grave. They had specific messages for me to give him. I promised that I would do so.

I hadn't been at his grave since last July, on the 1st anniversary of his passing. I wasn't looking forward to it this trip, not knowing what my emotions would be. I also wanted to do something special at his grave, something that I could tell Andrew and Ben about upon my return. But what?

As I pondered and prayed about it, I remembered the poignant scene from the movie *Schindler's List*, where scores of Jewish survivors passed by Oskar Schindler's grave, each with a stone in their left hand. They paused by the grave of the man responsible for saving their lives during the Holocaust, placed the stone on his grave, and walked away. The marker was covered with stones.

Why couldn't I do something similar for my husband's grave? An outdoorsman, he loved nature and simple things. I decided to bring a stone to his grave and leave it.

I cried all the way out to the cemetery, about a 12 mile drive from town. I prayed for strength to approach his grave. I hoped that I could make it a positive experience. I chose a stone from the church's gravel parking lot, placed it in my left hand, and walked to his marker. A cool breeze enveloped me, and I sat beside it, telling him about the wonderful exploits of his two sons. The subtle curve of the mausoleum top surprisingly held the stone in its place--so I returned to the parking lot for more. Searching for just the right colors, textures, and shapes, I came back with several, making myself at home, sitting on the mausoleum cover. In a few minutes I had shaped them into a lovely heart above his name. It. Is. Perfect.

I removed the hat I was wearing, one of his, with the Texas Parks and Wildlife Department logo, and placed it above the heart for photo purposes. This is what I will show his sons.

As soon as I was back at my computer, I Googled the Jewish tradition of placing stones on a grave. What I found was beautiful. Well before days of tombstones and carved markers, piles of stones covered graves out of necessity. The cairns kept the graves from being disturbed. Visitors to graves would bring a stone, place it on the grave with their left hands, as a sign of respect and remembrance. When others visit, the stones serve as a sort of calling card, showing that the deceased person's grave was visited.

They bear witness to the person's existence, their importance.

I showed the picture to my boys and explained the tradition. They thought the heart was lovely. Returning this week, they each picked a stone and walked to his graveside. Although I didn't cry much on my previous visit, I shed copious tears as I watched my sons place their stones within the heart I had fashioned and caressed their father's grave. Both took turns lying on the smooth granite surface. No young son or daughter should have to mourn a parent.

It. Breaks. My. Heart.

So, we "wait for hope to appear" as the scripture stated above. We had no choice but to "take it full-face", and have been doing so for almost two years.

Even at our worst, God is there. He never walks out. He never fails to return. He gives me the strength to wipe away my own tears, lean over my two sons, and gently, lovingly pick them up off of their daddy's grave.

As I hugged the younger one, telling him this grave is just the place his dad's earthly body is resting, the one that gave out on him, he tells me he feels his daddy standing right next to him. He reached out to hug the air beside him, and I smiled. Who am I to question the faith of a child? I, too, believed that Mark's spirit is there, right alongside God's. I imagined they were comparing notes on how much the boys have grown.

Dear Father in Heaven, Give mothers the courage, the wisdom, the grace, and the understanding to parent, even as their daddies are up in heaven with You. I will never be enough on my own, but with Your divine help and intervention, I can manage. Grant me the patience to stand strong in faith, waiting for hope to reappear. It will reappear, as You promised. In Your blessed Son's name I ask it all, Amen.

August 5
Promises
By Rene Zonner

> *Blessed is she who has believed*
> *that the Lord would fulfill His promises to her!"*
> Luke 1:45 NIV

August 8, 2010: On that evening, the life I had known for nearly fourteen years came to an end. I had no warning, no hints it was about to happen, and no time to prepare.

One minute I was living a normal and predictable life, and the next minute I was thrust into the unknown.

I was so scared those first few days, weeks, and months. I couldn't see beyond the present moment. I was consumed by the loss my children and I faced. I was scared about my finances, raising three kids is expensive. I worried about how I would function as an only parent. I feared my children would not grow up to be normal functioning adults without a father in their lives. I was convinced I would be alone for the rest of my life, never to be loved again.

These thoughts were so overwhelming that I begged God to give me some sort of assurance about the future. I just needed to know that it would be alright. I didn't need or even want the details right then. That wasn't what I was asking. I just needed Him to show me that I wasn't going to drown, even if I felt like I was.

So I asked, and God spoke. He spoke to my heart and told me that, just as He had in the past, He would provide for my family's financial needs. He reminded me that I can do all things in Christ…even single parenting. He comforted me with assurances that my children would be normal, well-adjusted adults. He soothed my fears by promising me that I would be loved again and have a good marriage if I just followed His lead.

That was three years ago, and I am seeing many of those promises being accomplished. We are financially stable even when so many widows are not. Being an only parent has been so challenging, but God has sent many people to us that have helped carry the burden and taken up some of the slack when I am overwhelmed. My children are doing well emotionally despite such a devastating loss. We have settled into our new normal, and life is good.

But I have to say that three years of widowhood has worn me down somewhat. I watch the small life insurance policy get smaller and I wonder if I will be able to stretch it until the kids are grown. I see that my kids still have so much growing up to do, and I succumb sometimes to that voice that says "You can't do this". I sit by myself at night after the kids go to bed, and the loneliness feels suffocating. Being a widow is hard and I am just plain tired.

I find myself doubting. Wondering if I really heard God whisper those promises to my heart. Satan asks me time and time again, "Did God really say…?" On my weak days I fall into the trap and I question if God did say it. I lose faith in the promises.

But then I found Luke 1:45. "Blessed is she who has believed that the Lord will fulfill His promises to her!" This verse is in the story of Mary sharing with her cousin Elizabeth what the angel told her. I have read this story many, many times, but that verse never stuck out to me. Until I needed to hear it! God's voice was so loud in my heart that He might as well have been speaking audibly. When I read that verse I knew that He was speaking to me. He was reminding me that I only have to believe.

When I focus on the promises, when I truly believe even when there is no reason to…I am blessed.

Dear friends, if you have been traveling this road for a while, you probably feel weary at times as well. If you haven't done so already, ask God to give you some promises for your future. And when He does, believe them. Believe them with all your heart. Our God does not lie. He always follows through. It may not be in your timing and it may not look like you expected but He will not fail you. Be blessed in the believing and trust Him. It's not always easy, and Satan will try to make you doubt, but I encourage you to stay strong and fight the lies with God's own words.

Father, Encourage me and remind me of the promises You have given each of us. Give me strength and power when Satan tries to make me question You. Help me to have patience and courage to wait for Your timing and to know that You always come through for me. Thank You, Lord, that You are the God of Truth and the God of Love. Thank You that I can count on whatever You have promised me. Amen

August 6
A Box I Did Not Choose
By Danita Hiles

When my husband Dave died six years ago – the hardest thing for me to get used to was the 'box marked widow'. I must have filled out five hundred forms during the paperwork process, and on every one had to check that box for marital status. Widow. Widow. WIDOW!!! Ugh. This word was (is) hard for me to embrace.

The government had decided this was my label. My bank. My doctor's office. My kid's school. My tax returns. Over and over again I was forced to check the box marked widow.

I wanted to scream – this is not me! This is not who I want to be. I want to be wife. Partner. Helpmate. Sister. Daughter. Mother . Friend.

Instead I was in a box. A box I didn't like. A box I didn't choose. A box marked 'widow'. Ugh.

In those early desperate days I asked God for something to hold onto from His word. I opened a devotional to a reading about Psalm 16 and the words literally jumped off the page at me. 'This is my portion and my cup' (vs. 5) . Essentially, in today's language – 'it is what it is'.

When the miracle doesn't happen and the doctor's news is grim and the relationship isn't restored and you are standing in a cemetery, sometimes it simply 'is what it is'. But oh, the sweet words of the next verse: 'He will make the boundaries fall for me in pleasant places...' In spite of today's ugly reality, we have His word on it that He alone is charge of the boundaries of our life. Nothing happens to us out of reach of His loving hand.

So then how do we walk through this valley ? The next few verses of Psalm 16 are pretty clear with three 'I wills' to guide us; I will always set the Lord before me... I will praise the LORD, who counsels me. And finally, because He is at my right hand, I will not be shaken. Even on difficult days like this early journal entry depicts:

Sometimes the feelings of grief and loneliness are so strong that I feel as though

I am drowning.

The impossibility of this day-to-day reality without Dave

Makes it even hard to breathe.

today it is a never ending frustration with things.

things that break.

things that cost money.

things that can't be fixed.

things that i am the only one responsible for cleaning and organizing and remembering.

There's only one grown-up in the house now
and she's really tired.
mommy, mommy, mommy,
can you? did you? would you?
thoughts of the future spiral ahead
will it be any different
one month
one year

five years from now?

will there be more mommy to go around?

will I finally have gotten a handle on this reality and become organized

and be the mature woman of God I have admired in others?

Will I ever come to grips with the word widow.

And single mother.

And always having leftovers because most recipes are designed to feed a family of four.

And we are no longer that.

God knows.

Tonight there is just me and these words

and His words to me

And when all else fails, and the world is crumbling,

I can stand on His word….

Six years later…I'm still standing!

Psalm 16 ends with this promise:

You have made known to me the path of life;

you will fill me with joy in your presence,

with eternal pleasures at your right hand.

Precious friends – we may never know the answer to life's hard questions, especially the whys of God's timing surrounding those we love. But He has promised us His joy on this earth and eternity with Him. My box still says widow , but my Bible says He is with me, and my future is in His hands. I choose to praise Him. I choose to set Him before me. I choose to allow him to fill me with joy in his presence and live out loud as long as I have breath!

August 7
Being Okay with Okay
By Liz Anne Wright

As Jesus and his disciples were on their way, he came to a village where a woman named Martha opened her home to him. She had a sister called Mary, who sat at the Lord's feet listening to what he said. But Martha was distracted by all the preparations that had to be made. She came to him and asked, "Lord, don't you care that my sister has left me to do the work by myself? Tell her to help me!"
"Martha, Martha," the Lord answered, "you are worried and upset about many things, but few things are needed—or indeed only one. Mary has chosen what is better, and it will not be taken away from her."

Luke 10:38-43 NIV

About seven years ago, I was trying to be Super-Mom. My days were filled with activity: homeschooling, church work, keeping a house, cooking, cleaning, and taking care of my husband and sons. My aim was to do the best that I could for my family ...all the time.

And I was doing okay managing all of this.

Not that I liked the word "okay." I viewed that word almost like defeat. I wanted to be described as doing a "fantastic," "awesome," or even "great" job. I identified much more with Martha in the Bible story than with her sister Mary.

Then my world was rocked, first by Keith's illness, then by his death.

And the word "okay" took on a whole new meaning.

At first, "okay" meant that I was surviving the grief, perhaps even making some progress with it. I was continuing to place one foot in front of the other. I was working out what I needed to with God spiritually and emotionally, and I was continuing to mother my children. We were moving forward as a family, taking one step at a time toward finding a "new normal."

The "Martha" Super-Mom days of the past were not a consideration at this. I was in survival mode. Okay was something to shoot for...something I *might* be able to achieve.

But over the five and a half years since Keith's death, I have learned a lot about being "okay."

I have realized that being "okay" is really a blessing from God.

Financially, we are "okay." I have been able to keep the house, and to continue to homeschool the boys, definite praises in this economy. This is a true testimony to the wisdom of Keith's financial planning...and to the graciousness of God's care for us as a family. While I may not have an "outstanding" financial position, we continue to be "okay."

The boys are "okay" as they continue to deal with the death of their dad, and the stresses of having just one (imperfect) parent. They are not plagued by anger or bitterness over their lives, but continue to seek God and see joy in their circumstances. The effect of the tragedy in their lives has been overall positive. Oh, they squabble, and argue, and sometimes disobey, but that is fine with me. In fact, it is a blessing. They are just normal, average kids. The best kind of "okay" to be!

My own relationship with God is "okay," as well. I do not blame Him for my lot in life. Even in the beginning, I did not spend time angry and turned away from Him, but instead, hurting, I turned in toward Him. As a result, my relationship with God is strengthened in ways it might not have been if I had not been through all of this. Being "okay" was my choice. God would have let me turn away from Him. I had that free will. I am so thankful that I was interested in making that relationship "okay" again, that He loved me enough to seek me in my hurt, to wrap His arms around me and offer me peace.

In fact, that is the only thing in my life that is not just "okay" – my God.

While I may be average or ordinary...just "okay"...*He* is not. The Bible describes Him as so much more:

Praise be to the Lord God, the God of Israel, who alone does marvelous deeds. Psalm 72:19:8 NIV

All this also comes from the Lord Almighty, whose plan is wonderful, whose wisdom is magnificent. Isaiah 28:29 NIV

For great is the LORD and most worthy of praise; He is to be feared above all gods. I Chronicles 16:25 NIV

I don't have to be more than "okay" because He is so much more than "okay." What a freeing thought!

Sisters, when we break ourselves away from the bondage of having to be more than we are, more than we were made to be...*when we can be happy with being "okay"*...we can rest wholly in Him and in His greatness...and glory in our own smallness. We don't have to carry the weight of the world on our shoulders. Praise God!

Father, thank You for my being "okay" and all You have done to help me be "okay". May I always be "okay" in You. In Jesus' name, Amen.

August 8
Dog on the Beach
By Danita Hiles

*Let the beloved of the Lord rest secure in Him,
for He shields Him all day long,
the beloved of the Lord rests securely between His shoulders.*
Deuteronomy 33:12 NIV

The sand on the Hawaiian beach was pure white, the sky above a brilliant blue, but with eyes squeezed shut to hold in the tears, I really didn't' see much of it. Waves were crashing on the shore but I couldn't hear much of it above my own sobs. The sand was soft and warm but I only knew that because I kept picking up handfuls and letting it run through my fingers to keep from screaming. It was a perfect Hawaiian day. And I was a perfect mess. In the past six weeks, I had made it through two funeral services for Dave, traveled from Honolulu to Pittsburgh to Tampa and back home to base housing in Hawaii.

Now it was time to pack up the house, move to the mainland with my girls and begin again. I guess leaving the last place we had lived together as a family was one more end of life as a 'we'. And the beginning of a lot more of 'I and 'me'. And that was really, really hard to imagine.

Eventually, though, I reached the end of my sobs and there was a quiet stillness in between the ragged breaths. Kind of a 'what now?' sense of expectation.

"Ok, Lord, here we are', I sniffed. 'And since it's just me and you, I really , really , really need to know you are with me'.

Being a dramatic kind of girl, I thought it would be just great if God would show off there on that beach and give me a sign. I mean a SIGN. Like maybe a school of dolphins frolicking in the waves. Or a gorgeous Hawaiian rainbow as a <u>right now</u> sign of His promises. I sat there on the sand with eyes still shut, There weren't any eloquent prayers, just a whispered 'Please, Jesus, help me', and a desperate hope that He would give me what I needed to make it through the next steps of this journey. I felt His peace wash over me and just knew I would open my eyes to see some sort of confirmation.

I slowly pried open my swollen eyes to check out the horizon. Nope, no school of dolphins there. I peered up into the sky, squinting to see if maybe, just maybe there was an edge of a rainbow, or a Holy Spirit dove shaped cloud (I told you I was desperate!). Nope, no rainbow, no dove.

But what was that weird noise? Kind of a huffy sort of wheeze over my right shoulder. I turned and there beside me on the sand was a dog. Not just a dog but a DOG, a big brown furry retriever of some sort. As I cocked my head at him, he took two steps closer and leaned up against me. And sighed. Wet fur and all.

And in that moment I felt like God kind of whispered to my heart,

'That's how close I am. Just as close as this wet dog leaning up against you. And we are going into the future together…just that close '.

I have thought of that dog so many times over the past few years. And smiled at God's sense of humor. And marveled at His closeness.

There may not be dolphins and rainbows, but we have the absolute assurance that no matter what happens, and no matter where our journey takes us, He is with us.

Not because we feel He is with us or we sense He is with us but simply because He has promised to be.

With us.

Emmanuel.

God with us.

I love that.

I pray you have a 'wet dog leaning up against you' closeness from Jesus today. He's that close.

August 9
Lonely, Yet Never Alone
By Nancy Howell

There is a time for everything,
and everything on earth has its special season.
There is a time to be born and a time to die.
There is a time to cry and a time to laugh.
There is a time to be sad and a time to dance.
There is a time to throw away stones and a time to gather them.
Ecclesiastes 3:1-2, 4 NCV

September 3, 2013. Just another day on the calendar for most, but not for me.

I have been dreading this day, wincing and squirming as it approaches. Wondering how in the wide world of sports I was going to get through the 24 hour period.

If my husband had lived, it would have been our 25th wedding anniversary.

So many memories. So much fun. A perfect day, way back in 1988, whenever I became Mrs. Mark Howell.

If I close my eyes, I can still see the look on his face as he saw me in my wedding dress for the first time.

I hear the music, see the church filled with family and friends. I see three Howell men (his father, younger brother, and himself) all a bit misty-eyed as the service gets underway.

I see my dad, as he nearly trips over my long train after giving my hand to his future son-in-law (by the way, it gave a great comic moment and set the tone for the ceremony).

So many years. So many memories. I never dreamed we would not see our 25th anniversary together.

We had plans (oh, if I had a dollar for every time I've written or proclaimed that sentence!). Graduate student budgets allowed for a Florida honeymoon while we pipe dreamed of Hawaii. A pact was made, early in the marriage. We would spend our 25th in Hawaii, and leave our boys with the two grandmas.

But you know the way those plans ended-- with me becoming a widow over two years ago.

My boys and I have made great strides. We are committed to moving forward and living life to the fullest, because we know in our hearts that's what their daddy wants for us.

That doesn't make it any easier.

I look back and see how far we have come. I look ahead and see there are miles and miles to go.

For now, though, all I can see is September 3rd on my day planner.

I awake early that morning, well before sunrise. I think back to my wedding day. I had done the same thing.

Twenty-five years ago, I was young, head over heels in love, getting ready to start the greatest adventure of my life. I felt all-encompassing joy from head to toe.

This year? Astonishingly enough, as the memories flooded my mind, and my morning prayers took flight, I felt more grateful than I did sad.

There were tears throughout the day, for sure, but they were not all sad and grief-filled. I smiled a lot. I told our sons several wedding day stories about their daddy. And I made it through.

There is a time to mourn. Heaven knows I have done my share and then some. There is also a time to laugh. And live.

I am ready for my new season of laughing, knowing full well that there will still be periods in which I cry.

What season do you find yourself in today, dear one? Are you in the mind-numbing shock of recent loss, where you cannot even remember what day it is?

Tomorrow I will tell you about the comfort I have received from Jesus Christ.

Dear God in Heaven, Thank You for helping me on the days that are the hardest. You are the only comfort that is eternal. Help me to go to You today for that comfort. Amen

August 10
Lonely, Yet Never Alone Continued
By Nancy Howell

I was telling you about dealing with my 25th wedding anniversary as a widow yesterday. I was ready for a new season of laughing instead of only tears. I wanted to live again. Where do you find yourself today?

Are you angry at being left alone?

Do you rewind the events of your loved one's passing over and over and over, playing out "should have/would have/could have" scenarios on a continuous loop in your head?

Have you hit a wall, spiritually and or emotionally, where you are pretty certain you cannot go one step farther along this path alone?

Are you overwhelmed with all of the added responsibilities the loss has put square on your slight shoulders, from yard work to balancing the checkbook to changing the oil in your car to making life decisions?

Maybe you find yourself now a single parent, dealing with not only your loss, but also the devastation of your children being without their dad?

Whatever the season you are in, right at this very moment, I want you to know:

You. Are. Not. Alone.

Did you get that? You are not in this mess by yourself.

First of all, you have God. And Jesus. And the Holy Spirit, who is interceding on your behalf between your earthly turmoil and heaven.

Next, you have us.

We are here for you, albeit in a small way, right here at A Widow's Might. Women on this team are in different seasons of life, different seasons of widowhood...but we all "get it." We've walked where you are walking.

We've probably cried as many tears. We've most likely spent sleepless nights, wondering how God could ever redeem a terrible situation and bring some good from it.

But He, and He alone, can. And He will.

You just have to let Him in.

I made it through my anniversary, with God by my side.

My eleven year old, wiser than his earthly years, said it better than I ever could: "Mom, I want you to not be too sad today. We are doing really well. God and Dad know that."

Dear God in Heaven, Give me the reassurance that whatever season I am in today, I will continue to heal if I just focus my eyes and heart on You. You know my needs before I even ask. I pray for peace, for comfort, and for guidance as I re-align my life. Show me Your plans for me. In Jesus' name, Amen.

August 11
A Detour?
By Leah Stirewalt

As we tiptoe closer to those often-marked events that can wreak havoc in the life of a grieving widow, I'm reminded of a place I found myself this time last year. A place I had to stop and ponder – several times over – whether or not I belonged there or was truly there to begin with.

The place?

The Road of Healing.

I had been trudging along what I still dub, Grief Road, going through the motions of my new normal. I had some good days and many, many bad days, but I could see a gradual change in the good vs. the bad. Overall, I felt I was doing pretty well, considering having gone through the loss of my husband to suicide within the past year. I honestly didn't know where I was on Grief Road, but I knew that I could sense God healing me…in His own way, and in His own timing BUT with my determination and deep desire to allow Him to do it.

So, what caused me to stop and ponder on that definitive day around this time last year, when I felt my two roads – Grief Road and The Road of Healing – had converged? It was the feeling of being sucker-punched. Suddenly – I felt as if my world had stopped, yet again. To me, it seemed as if it came out of nowhere. But, I vividly remember the realization I felt when I noticed the holiday season was coming up quickly, and I would not be spending it with my sweet husband that year. Oh, the ache I felt at that sudden insight.

I began to wobble on that supposed Road of Healing. Suddenly, I felt I had taken a detour along a new road. It looked similar to Grief Road, but yet different. I felt so unsure on this new road and so shaky. I felt I was a foreigner on very unforgiving soil. I began to listen to my own thoughts…

> *You have a long way to go.*
> *You've had a setback in your healing.*
> *You're nowhere where you thought you were.*
> *See? The grieving process will never end.*

Oh, the thoughts! The ugly, self-defeating thoughts.

Thankfully, with the help of some friends, I began to see the <u>untruths</u> of those thoughts. Yes – it was a very difficult time that had just crested in my life. The waves were going to be crashing again. But, they don't last forever. Just like the waves in the ocean can't stay in one place forever, this place of pain would also not last. It was very difficult, but I found walking directly into that place of pain, rather than trying to avoid it, actually helped me to get to the other side even more healed than I was when I began.

A setback? Hardly! I was being way too hard on myself. It was all a normal part of the process. I just had to come to that realization myself. It's okay to be moving along The Road of Healing to discover a momentary detour. It's okay to cry…to scream…to feel deep loneliness…to be angry…a whole host of other emotions on this detour. Just don't get off the detour and make your own path. Keep moving…keep walking, and if you simply can't walk right now…allow God to carry you. He just wants you to ask.

Isaiah 4216 (NIV 1984)…
I will lead the blind by ways they have not known,
along unfamiliar paths I will guide them;
I will turn the darkness into light before them
and make the rough places smooth.
These are the things I will do;
I will not forsake them.

August 12
I Have a Purpose
By Sheryl Pepple

I now understand what it feels like to be "a fish out of water"; gasping for oxygen and thinking I was going to die. I have learned that there actually is a medical condition known as "broken heart syndrome" in which there is a swelling around the walls of your heart that, if you were to get an MRI during that time, it would be impossible to distinguish it from a heart attack. I know, because for months after the State Troopers showed up at my door to tell me my husband had been killed, I felt like I was having a heart attack and I was gasping for survival. Occasionally, those feelings can return and it always surprises me. I have noticed that it tends to happen when I have to introduce myself to someone new and they ask me about my family. I am no longer a wife, raising a family. My kids are grown and have moved away. My husband is with the Lord. What then is my purpose?

The Lord has been good to me. He has prepared me for this season in my life. Thirteen years ago He planted an insatiable hunger in my heart for Him. I started really studying His Word and through His Word I really started to get to know Him. I am so grateful that He pulled me into biblical community with other believers. It started with a neighborhood bible study group, and then He prompted me to volunteer at my church as a leader for Women's discipleship. Over the years I have become more and more invested in His church and eventually I was asked to join staff as the director of Small Groups. All along the journey He surrounded me with people who encouraged me in studying His Word. The night the State Troopers appeared at my door I was leading a Bible study on the names of God. That very night we were studying about El-Shaddai – the All Sufficient One. Oh, how I have learned about my God, El-Shaddai.

I remember worrying about so many things those first few days, weeks, and months. All of which El Shaddai covered. El Shaddai gave me the wisdom and strength to handle what I needed. He also provided others to help support me along the way. I worried so much about not being able to carry "my load" in my job but El Shaddai provided people to encourage me so that in my weakness they could see Him.

As I continue to walk this journey, new opportunities have started to appear. El Shaddai has given me the strength to keep walking and to try new things. Writing to you is one of these "new things". It is something I would have never imagined, but something I am so grateful for. I have discovered it is one more piece in fulfilling my purpose – of teaching and proclaiming the good news that Jesus is the Christ.

Dear Heavenly Father, Thank You so much for being my El Shaddai – my All Sufficient One. Thank you for guiding me, comforting me, providing for me and for having a purpose for me. Thank You, Father, that You are my creator and I am Your creation, fearfully and wonderfully made. Thank You, most of all for Your Son who is the Christ who lived and died and rose again so that I could have eternal life. In your Son's Holy and Precious name, Amen.

August 13
Reflections
By Karen Emberlin

> *But those who trust in the Lord will find new strength.*
> *They will soar high on wings like eagles.*
> *They will run and not grow weary.*
> *They will walk and not faint.*
> *Isaiah 40:31 NLT*

As I look at the past twenty months of my "unwanted journey" as a widow, I must admit I am surprised I have come this far. The journey has not been easy, but God has been there every step of the way and blessed me in so many ways I did not think were possible. However, I am finding as life begins to settle into a new "normal" routine, the reality is beginning to sink in that my husband is gone and will never again be a part of my life here on earth! I know that I must find the courage to accept what cannot be changed and continue on – I *know* Don would not want me to be sad the rest of my life, he would want me to be happy, but how do I move on and overcome this reality and the loneliness?

I recently saw and fell in love with the Willow Tree® angel "Soar – A Time To Reflect, A Time To Soar". Susan Lordi describes her creation with these words: *"At significant milestones, we often pause and reflect before moving forward."*

Reflect and Move Forward! What would my husband want me to remember and what would he encourage me to do in order to move on without him?

Smile - He would tell me to "smile" – He said I always looked so much better when I was smiling! Don and I had our own business and spent many hours together working on the computer. When things did not go "just right" I could get discouraged very easily and lose my smile. One morning after struggling with a project the previous day, I found this "sticky note" on my computer as a reminder of not only his love and support but God's love for me and to keep smiling!

Remember Us - I know without a doubt my husband would want me to never forget the 48 years we shared together . Yes, there were "bumps in the road", we were not perfect, but with God's help we survived the bumps and loved each other more each day as the years passed. We were looking forward to "growing old" together. I miss Don so much and no one will ever replace him – the love we had was ours and nothing can take that away!

Never Give Up - He would emphasize that I was to never give up or quit – even when I doubt myself. Don was always so positive and never gave up! For many years there was a plaque on his desk with the poem Don't Quit – some of the lines include; *"When care is pressing you down a bit, rest if you must, but don't you quit." "So stick to the fight when you're hardest hit – It's when things seem worst that you mustn't quit".* The plaque is now on my dresser, next to our picture, as a reminder from him to never quit!

Pray For Our Family – Don prayed daily for our children and grandchildren. He would want me to continue this legacy of prayer. He would also want me to love them and stay close to them, even though we are many miles apart.

Trust God For Everything - When we faced tough situations I would say to him, "What are we going to do"? His reply was always "God will take care of us – we just need to pray about it and trust Him". Don was the strong one and he knew I was the weak one so he tried hard to take care of me. Now, without him, he would want me to lean on the Father. God also knows I am weak and He is there to take care of me. He knows I need to depend on Him to get through each day. The verse in Isaiah 40:31 reminds us we will find new strength if we trust in the Lord – we can soar and run and not grow weary – what a promise!!

Tough to live up to some days, but by the grace of God, I can and will continue to move forward.

I know there will still be many challenges in the coming days. There will still be days when the "waves of grief" will roll in at unexpected times. However, I know without a doubt Don would want me to cherish our memories and never forget them, and he would want me to "smile" often and "go on"!

Lord, You know the hurt I feel in my heart from the loss of my husband. Help me to cherish the memories, but also to trust You daily for the new strength You promise me. May I not grow weary, but soar like eagles and run the race You have put before me. Amen

August 14
Guess You'll Have to Find Something Else to be Afraid of...
By Kit Hinkle

Benaiah the son of Jehoiada, the son of a valiant man of Kabzeel, who had done many acts; he slew two lion-like men of Moab: also he went down and slew a lion in a **pit** *in a* **snowy** *day.*

1 Chronicles 11:22

Years ago, long before I was widowed, before I was even married to Tom, life threw a huge dose of pain my way. A marriage I thought was going to last me a lifetime went into a tailspin when an anonymous caller tipped me off to my first husband's affair.

At that horrible moment, I would never have imagined how the Lord was preparing the way for a new life, a new marriage, and strengthening me for a far deeper loss by teaching me never to fear being alone.

My first reaction was to drop the receiver and dash out of my office into the cool October air to catch my breath.

I didn't stop there. I got in my car and drove away, beating back tears. With nowhere to go, I stopped at a phone booth and called Joyce—my no-nonsense, stay cool through any storm friend.

I sobbed over the betrayal. "This is my worst fear and now it's happened!"

There was a pause on the other end while I knew Joyce prayed over what words to use. The ones that slipped off her tongue might strike you as uncaring or rude, but they were perfect. "Well, I guess you'll just have to find something else to be afraid of."

I wiped my tears and let her words sink in. All those years I tried to be the best wife to that man, but secretly harbored a sense that he had one foot out the door. Was I making every decision to please him out of faith or fear? What wasted time and effort! Had I faced my fear and stopped placating to him, he might have respected me more and considered changing his heart towards making a strong marriage. Or maybe not, but at least I would have been operating as the complete woman God made me to be and not have a nagging feeling that my jellyfish spine had something to do with my marriage falling apart.

But how about now, as we find ourselves widowed? Are we avoiding our worst fears and setting ourselves up for future regret?

When people ask "what's your worst fear?" Some of us think of loss or trauma, but if we're honest, sometimes it isn't the big stuff that we fear the most. After all, as widows, we've already experienced some of the worst. Our real fears are rooted in insecurity, wondering if we're good enough or accepted.

When Joyce told me I need to find something else to be afraid of, I chose God. I never wanted anything in life to shake me to the core like the betrayal from my first husband did. I wanted to be absolutely positive that I knew who I was at the core of my being so whatever is going on around me, I still feel accepted, cherished, powerful.

And I do. Oh, the deceiver tries to scare that sense of confidence away, but I know the signs of his presence. It's that gnawing anxiety…. I'm alone, I'm overwhelmed, my kids don't have a father, I can't do this, are the kids getting what they need? Am I messing up? Will I ever find another companion to grow old with?

In my Bible lessons this week I learned about a great soldier of David's named Benaiah. He was courageous. Courage means doing what needs to be done in spite of your fears.

So back to the anxieties. They whirl and whirl, and then I say…

Stop.

These are feelings. They aren't truth. I stop, and I refocus on Scripture. On truth. I am incredible and loved in the Lord. Through Him, I'm unstoppable, because He does all I can't. He will be the father of my boys, my husband. He cherishes me and loves me and I will respond with obedience. I will ignore the anxious thoughts—endure them as a sort of pain like a steady leg cramp and get to work… one foot in front of the other. I will act accordingly to His grace. I will do all those things I would do as if I were loved and cherished, not because I feel loved or cherished, but because I know I am loved and cherished. It's truth, and I believe it, so my feet and hands and mouth follow my beliefs, in spite of any lingering anxiety the deceiver tosses at me.

I stop pacing the house and grab a deck of cards and hang out with the boys. I pull out five bibles—one for each of us, put on some Christian music, and have quiet reading time in the Word with the boys followed by prayers.

And guess what, the boys LOVE it. "Thanks, Mom. Can we do this every day?" My heart fills with centered clean joy. I'm back. I remembered who I am.

The world sees widow, but when I remember who I am, in that moment, I'm not the pitiful widow. I'm Kit, a woman of God.

Lord, I ask You to lift me up and show me how powerful I am in the cover of my obedience to You. Walk me through my fear, and teach me that complete potential to display Your glory lies on the other side when I face and conquer my anxieties. In Your Son's Heavenly Name I pray. Amen

August 15
Needs Supplied
By Elizabeth Dyer

And my God will meet all your needs,
according to His glorious riches in Christ Jesus.
Philippians 4:19NIV

What does this verse mean to me or you in our widowhood? Our pastor spoke on this verse recently and it really got me thinking. I did some internet searching about the verse and the context, causing me to ask myself some tough questions.

The context of the verse is that the Philippian people supplied the Apostle Paul's needs according to their <u>poverty</u> and God would supply their needs according to His <u>riches</u>. So maybe in generosity to <u>others,</u> God provides for the <u>giver.</u> I guess we have to trust God that we will have enough when we give away what isn't ours in the first place. When we give, we are showing our faith.

Other questions started coming to light. Is the verse only referring to spiritual needs that are met or actual financial needs? According to today's economic standards? When Jesus fed the '5000' (plus) in the New Testament, there was an abundance of leftovers. Is that what I should be expecting? Or can I even consider that as a possibility?

I often think of the orphan home director from 19th century England, George Muller. He never told anyone of the needs of the orphanage and God always provided milk, bread, and all their of supplies. He is credited with this quote: "The beginning of anxiety is the end of faith, and the beginning of true faith is the end of anxiety." Do I have enough faith in God to sit down at an empty table, full of children and say our prayer for dinner, believing God will provide? Have I ever tried that? Have I ever allowed God to provide in that way?

The Amplified Version of this verse says that God will "liberally supply (fill to the full) your every need". In thinking about my situation, and the desire of my heart is to concentrate on just being a single parent while helping other widows with young children, is it fair for me to think God would possibly bring money in to pay our bills? From sources unknown?

The financial advice I keep getting is to work and invest and make money to take care of my family for the future. But my heart tells me to stay home and not work and be as involved as I can with my kids in their schools. In ten years, I don't want to regret the time I spent making money instead of spending time with them.

Both directions are good, but what does God want me to?

For now, I have decided to stretch my faith by not working outside the home. This probably seems like foolishness to some but God has put this on my heart to do. I believe that if He has called me, He will provide for me.

This is my journey. Yours may look very different. That is the beauty of the Christian walk. It looks different for everyone but the end goal of maturing in our faith is the outcome. Don't live like me. Live like God leads you.

My God.

Will meet.

All my needs.

According to His glorious riches in Christ Jesus.

This is personal, folks. My God. My needs. Your God. Your needs.

Heavenly Father, I pray today that I can know a peace that only You can give. I want to believe that You will provide for all my needs but I struggle with unbelief. Give me confidence when I doubt. Give me strength when I feel weak. I want to walk in faith with You today. Thank You for Your continued grace in my life. Amen

August 16
Progressing Past Pity
By Liz Anne Wright

As He passed by, He saw a man blind from birth. And His disciples asked Him, "Rabbi, who sinned, this man or his parents, that he would be born blind?" Jesus answered, "It was neither that this man sinned, nor his parents; but it was so that the works of God might be displayed in him.

John 9:1-3NIV

The man answered and said to them, "Well, here is an amazing thing that you do not know where He is from, and yet He opened my eyes. We know that God does not hear sinners; but if anyone is God-fearing and does His will, He hears him. Since the beginning of time it has never been heard that anyone opened the eyes of a person born blind. If this man were not from God, He could do nothing."

John 9:30-33NIV

The other night, I went to dinner with some of my widow friends. We got to talking about the way people react to us, what they expect from us as widows.

My friend told a story about seeing a woman she had not seen in a while. This woman exhibited classic pity for her and her kids at their situation…and was almost offended when my friend was not as sad as she was.

I guess it is understandable. She walks on the path of grief, by choice, a few times a year. We live here…day in and day out…not by choice.

We have a completely different perspective.

Instead of accumulating our days in the arena battling grief one at a time, over a long period of time, we accumulate them day in, day out, and month upon month. It is bound to take us to a different place than those around us. They punch out of the time clock for periods of time. We never do.

And in so doing, we progress. We have to.

The problem is when the world around us expects us to punch their clock with them, to step back to the time of grief where they are, instead of speeding up with us. Since they do not live with the grief daily, they don't progress as we do.

And it is often awkward, uncomfortable, and even stressful, to be near them.

I bet it was so for this blind man in Jesus' day as well.

Everyone who saw him immediately went to a place of pain and ugliness…thinking he had sinned to be in that condition, or his parents had, for him to be facing the world blind.

But Jesus came…and told him and all those around him that he was blind in order to *show God's might*.

And right away, this recently-healed man had the opportunity to witness…to everyone…including the Pharisees!

I think that is the way we need to look at the situation with those who pull us back into the pit, who expect us to take a step back in our progress in order to satisfy their need to give us pity.

We need to carefully, lovingly educate them on grief.

In a culture largely uneducated about grief and its workings, I think we have to expect that people will not understand how we live…how we can progress past the pity to joy and a full life again. We, as a culture, are too tied up in life here on earth, and are often not looking beyond to life in Heaven.

But we have this opportunity, as the healed-blind man did, to point others to the Author of our healing and to His plan for our life…and our death. And this can be accomplished in a few easy steps.

- Give them grace when they don't get it. They can't possibly know how you feel. They have not been there. But that doesn't mean they aren't trying.

- Realize that there is a God-given opportunity here. All of us face grief at some times in our lives; perhaps you can give them a gift in the form of education that can help them deal with their own grief better when the time comes.

- Patiently, lovingly, lead them to understand grief better. I know it is often difficult to talk about the journey we are on…but if the Lord desires it, He will give you the strength to get through it, and the words to say.

I pray we will *all* have the strength to deal with these situations as God would have us…for His greater glory.

Dear Father, this journey is often hard enough without odd encounters and people who would pull me back. Please give me strength to deal with all of those who I meet and must tell of my life story with grace and love. Help me to help them when You desire it, but not be pulled back into the pit of grief. Thank

You for loving me, and pulling me from the place of pity. In Jesus' name, Amen.

August 17
Clothe Yourself
By Sheryl Pepple

Therefore, as God's chosen people,
holy and dearly loved,
clothe yourselves with compassion, kindness, humility,
gentleness, and patience.
Bear with each other and forgive whatever grievances you may
have against one another.
Forgive as the Lord forgave you.
And over all these virtues put on love,
which binds them all together in perfect unity.
Colossians 3:12-14 NIV

I have had so many of those moments in the last five months. You know those moments, when you just get so irritated with people. You can't believe what they said or didn't say. You can't believe what they did or didn't do. You want to scream…don't you understand how much pain I'm in???? One of the many things that God has spoken to me through my minister was the answer to that very question…no they don't get it and they are not supposed to.

Fortunately, probably most of the people we know or come in contact with have not experienced the depth of pain that we go through when we lose our spouse. But then, most have also never experienced the depth of God's love, compassion, and provision that we are experiencing, either.

It is so important that we give ourselves grace during this time. There are days, weeks, months, when we walk around in a fog. There are many, many times when we are irritable, and every day we struggle to deal with our loss. But more important than giving ourselves grace, it is powerful to remember that God has given us grace. Grace when we didn't deserve it. Grace that covers absolutely everything we could possibly think, say or do. Grace because He loves us more than we can begin to comprehend. I am so grateful that none of the things I have thought or said these last few months stand between me and my God, whom I so desperately need. His Son has already paid for every one of our sins on the Cross and we can call out to our God with confidence. Our sin is as far away from us as the east is from the west (Psalms 103:12).

It is because of His Grace that the Holy Spirit lives in us once we believe. And it is through the power of the Holy Spirit that we are able to clothe ourselves with compassion, kindness, humility, gentleness and patience. It is why when someone does or says the wrong thing, we are, if we choose, able to respond with kindness and extend grace to them. It isn't always our natural response, but through Him it is possible. And each time we clothe ourselves with compassion, kindness, humility, gentleness and patience, we have the privilege of letting others see Christ living in us!

Dear Heavenly Father, Thank You so much for loving me and covering me with Your grace! Thank You for the sacrifice of

Your Son who died on the Cross for me. Thank You for the Holy Spirit who guides me and comforts me! Please help me to remember every day the gift of Your grace and help me to clothe myself in compassion, kindness, humility, gentleness and patience. Father, let others see You living in me, that You may be glorified! Amen

August 18
The Gift of Singleness?
By Rene Zonner

*Each one should use whatever gift he has received
to serve others, faithfully administering God's grace
in its various forms.*

1 Peter 4:10

I have heard my pastor several times in the past few years talk about the "gift of singleness". Quite frankly, I thought he was crazy. I remember thinking the first time I heard it, how easy it was for him to think of it as a gift when he has been married for forty years. As someone who had it thrust upon her unwillingly, I was having a hard time seeing what was so great about it

In the early months of my widowhood I remember being worried that people would think I was divorced if they saw me alone with the kids. I practically wore a sign around my neck announcing I was a widow rather than let people think I was unmarried by choice or divorce. I look back on that now and just shake my head. The desire to have my old life back, to still be able to say I was a married woman was taking up space in my heart that should have been desiring God. It was hard to tell when I had crossed the line into desiring a status more than missing the man who was my husband, but I had.

About six months after John died, I felt God asking me why I was still wearing my wedding rings. I told myself that it was because they were a reminder of John and our time together and because I still considered myself his wife. But God knew better. He knew that, by this time, I was wearing my rings because I didn't want to have a visible reminder that I was no longer married. I didn't want to stick out as being different from all my married friends. I didn't want strangers making assumptions about my life. It was for all the wrong reasons, so I took them off. I haven't worn a ring of any kind on that finger since then.

I was moving into acceptance that I was single but I didn't really have any single friends. I had been married for fourteen years and I was forty years old….my circle naturally just did not include a lot of single people anymore. So I decided it was time to seek out other singles and not necessarily widows. I needed others who had embraced their singleness and were thriving.

I am blessed that my church has a singles group for adults in their thirties and forties so I went and checked it out. It was hard. I didn't want to be there and I was the only widow. But now, two years later, I can see what a big and important step that was. I had finally accepted my new status and was on my way to embracing singleness. I now have a wonderful group of single friends who are giving me love and support as we travel this road together. And if you want total honesty…there is some fun in being single.

I've learned to see the gifts of my singleness. I can have close (unmarried) male friends again. Married women don't get to hang out with the guys. I can make decisions without having to consult someone. What I say goes. I have learned that sprawling out in the middle of the bed makes it feels more spacious. I don't have to share closet space. Chick flick marathon? Yes, please! And then there is dating again. A bit nerve racking at times but exciting as well and full of possibilities.

The most important gift of my singleness is that I can be used for ministry in ways I couldn't while married. When my husband was still here, I turned down some serving opportunities because they would have taken away from the time I had to spend with him. Now I am freed up a bit more. I can be used by God in ways and in areas I couldn't before being single again. I am able to use this gift for however long God gives it to me to focus on others and devote myself to his work in a way not possible while married.

Embracing my singleness did not happen quickly and the process began only after I had done the hard work of getting to the other side of my grief. Only you will know when you are ready for this step but I encourage you to think about it. When you are ready, search out other singles. Learn from those who are embracing the single life. Ask God to show you what gifts he has for you as a single adult. You might be surprised what you find!

Father, Show me that in every season of my life, You have a gift to give if I just open my heart to it. Lord, I ask that You bring people into my life who will walk with me in singleness. Give me insight as to what new opportunities You have in store for me that can only be realized as a single. Help me to embrace the "gift of singleness". Amen

August 19
I Can't
By Sherry Rickard

And Isaac spake unto Abraham his father, and said, ... Behold the fire and the wood; but where is the lamb for a burnt offering? And Abraham said, My son, God will provide himself a lamb for a burnt offering: so they went both of them together. And they came to the place which God had told him of, and Abraham built an altar there and laid the wood in order, and bound Isaac his son and laid him on the alter upon the wood. And Abraham stretched forth his hand, and took the knife to slay his son. And the angel of the Lord called unto him out of heaven, and said, Abraham... Lay not thine hand upon the lad, neither do thou anything unto him... And Abraham lifted up his eyes, and looked, and behold behind him a ram caught in a thicket by his horns: and Abraham went and took the ram, and offered him up for a burnt offering in the stead of his son.

Genesis 22: 7-13 KJV

Silence. Nausea. Disbelief. Relief. Sadness. Loneliness. Confusion. Emptiness. These are the emotions I began to experience on the afternoon I lost my husband in Durham, North Carolina. The

Lord was there with me that day, but, for a moment I turned my face from Him and walked away. He had asked me to take something I loved with all my heart and sacrifice it. Give it to Him and trust that it would all be ok. I walked all the way to the altar, put my beloved on it, praying the whole time he would be spared. It didn't happen, my beloved was called home. And in the silent, empty world I now lived in, a thought kept repeating itself in my head until I couldn't breathe, "I can't do this." How can you continue to be alive when your heart has been ripped from your chest? Yet there I was, still breathing, still thinking. My eyes had the ability to blink and focus. I felt like the walking dead and, without my Savior, I was like a walking dead person. I have never felt so utterly alone before.

How could He have asked this of me? You don't answer someone's prayer and give them their soul mate and then, when their love is so solid and founded in You, take them Home. That's not how it works. This was my thought pattern as I packed up my things from my hotel room near the hospital, as I drove home from North Caroline to Virginia, as I accepted the home-cooked meals, planned the funeral, bought the casket and burial plot. "I can't do this..."

When we went down to Duke for his bone marrow transplant, we had to meet with a social worker. She asked us what our biggest fear was. My fear was that I would have to drive home without him. "I can't do this..."

Thankfully, I have a very close relationship with my Savior and I was surrounded by people who loved the Lord. During this time, they carried me and my needs to the throne room, when I couldn't bear to think about my Savior.

It has been almost three years since Bill went Home and, not only have I done "this", but I can tell you I am living victoriously through Christ. I understand that God, in calling Bill Home, made the most loving, best decision for everyone.

I have also learned that I REALLY "can't do this..." God has never intended for us to do "this" alone. He wants fellowship with us. He wants us to come to Him with everything. He wants us to rely on Him for everything. I have learned to accept the Grace and Mercy He gives me every morning and just use it for today. He is faithful and will give me more for tomorrow. I can't do this in me, but if I surrender and lose me, He is made bigger in me and things just work out.

It hasn't been an easy road, but on every step of this journey, God has lovingly wrapped His arms around me and listened to every thought I had and never left my side. I don't want to do this, but God needs me to walk this journey. Each day, I grow stronger in Him and I see that He provides for all my needs.

Thank You, Lord, for loving me so much and walking this journey with me. Amen

August 20
My Widow's Mite
By Nancy Howell

Jesus sat down opposite the treasury, where people came to bring their offerings, and He watched as they came and went. Many rich people threw in large sums of money, but a poor widow came and put in only two small coins worth only a fraction of a cent.

Jesus *(calling His disciples together):* " *Truly this widow has given a greater gift than any other contribution. All the others gave a little out of their great abundance, but this poor woman has given God everything she has."*

Mark 12:41-44 Voice

The story of a widow's mite. We're all familiar with it. The widow gives two small coins, in the midst of a congregation of rich people. Note the rich "threw" in large sums of money, while the widow simply "put" her offering in the coffer. And yet, Jesus tells the disciples that she has given the greater gift. All others gave a little out of their great stores, but she gave God everything she had.

Wow.

The play on the words "mite" and "might" have great meaning for me. Finding this website in December 2011, a mere six months after I became a widow, was truly a Godsend and a lifeline. Here is a place that finally "gets" me. These women have walked in my shoes.

So whenever I had the opportunity to purchase a small sterling silver charm, that of a widow's mite, from my favorite Texas jeweler, James Avery, I was ecstatic. I think I bought the first charm in the Wichita Falls store inventory, early 2012. I put the charm on my new necklace, alongside the "Best Mom" charm given to me by my boys that first Christmas without their dad.

I rarely took that necklace off, wearing it for months on end. Now I know that little charm had no great powers, but I felt stronger when I had it on. Whenever my faith would waver, or I would come up against a situation I had no clue how to deal with (and those still come around fairly often), I would reach up to my throat and finger that charm, nestled so snugly up against the other. I ran my fingers over its two carved sides, slowed down to breathe, and usually whispered a little prayer for "might from the mite" from God.

It became my signature look. Most photos taken of me show it front and center.

I thought I would never take it off.

But over the course of the past few months, beginning around the two-year mark of my becoming a widow, I found myself reaching for it less. Call it healing, or more self-assurance, if you wish. I call it natural growth and the progression of life as God wants me to live it.

I quit wearing it as often. It began to be rotated out with other favorite pieces, which I had not worn since before my husband's death. A heart with a mother and baby in the middle. A delicate small cross with diamonds. And numerous other James Avery pieces that I had collected through the years.

Do you have something that is a symbol of your status as a widow? Some have a necklace or a bracelet. Some have a pin. Others have a piece of their husband's jewelry that they wear.

Tomorrow I will tell you what happened after two years of being a widow. My healing took me through growth to another stage.

August 21
My Widow's Mite Part 2
By Nancy Howell

I began telling you yesterday about the charm I bought right after my husband passed away. And I told you how I wore it as my signature jewelry. But then the two year mark came and I began to wear it less and less.

That charm still holds much significance for me, don't get me wrong, but I think I am ready to take the next step. I have a charm bracelet that I began after my husband's death. I decided to put charms on it that signified important events in our combined lives. On it there are, in no particular order, two boy charms with our sons' names and birthdates, a Kansas sunflower (his birth state, and where he is buried), a large-mouth bass (he was a fisheries biologist and taught me how to fish), a shotgun (to commemorate his love of hunting, and my picking up that same love to share with our son), a deer (which always makes an appearance for us when we are on our Kansas land), a memorial heart (inscribed with his name, a dash, and an infinity sign), and a cabin (to signify the cabin that we are beginning to build on that family land).

There's a spot I have saved on that bracelet for my widow's mite. Deep back in the recesses of my mind, I hoped there would be a day whenever I could symbolically remove the charm from my neck. I hoped I would be able to solder it to the bracelet.

I wasn't ready until now to even think of this change. The charm on the necklace could be moved from chain to chain, mixed with others, or worn on its own. But putting it on the bracelet was more permanent. Once there, it would stay, unless I took it back to the jewelry store.

I prayed so hard about this seemingly simple decision. Moving the charm would symbolize a new chapter in my life. I will always be Mark Howell's widow. It is a badge I have worn with honor, and, hopefully, dignity for the better part of two years. I miss him countless times a day, every day, and will for the rest of my earthly life. I see him in our sons, I hear him in their laughter. Everywhere I look I see his love for me and his boys.

But time keeps on slipping, slipping, slipping...into the future (with my apologies to the Steve Miller Band).

I am finally ready to move the charm to its permanent home.

With the symbolic move, I am also ready to take the badge of widowhood from around my neck, incorporating it into the rest of my persona, right alongside Kentucky native, outdoor lover, A.J. and Ben's mom, blogger, writer, speaker, and Jesus girl. I may always be a widow, but I would rather be known as someone who chose to live and live well, despite her circumstances.

For me, it is a natural progression, a "next step" in my walk.

I hope to love again someday, if it's in God's plan. I want to continue to grow, evolve, learn, and make a real difference in this world with the rest of the life God sees fit to give me.

Encouraging widows will always be a part of that, but I want to spread my wings on a wider scale. I am living, breathing proof that God can bring good out of a whole lot of bad.

Dear sisters, don't be discouraged if you aren't at this point yet. You will get there, in God's time.

And His timing is perfect. In the meantime, surround yourself with good friends, God's word, and fully trust in God's ability to heal you for a beautiful next chapter.

Dear Father in heaven, We are all at different stages of grief and loss, coming to You with different financial situations, and family dynamics that may not be the best. But I come to you in need. Help me. Prepare me to live again. You and only You are capable of enabling me to turn the page, to begin the next chapter of my life. Your grace is enough. It will always be enough. Teach me patience, endurance, and above all show me that life is still good in the midst of this bad I've been given. In Jesus' name I ask it all, Amen.

August 22
Game Changers
By Elizabeth Dyer

Then you will know which way to go,
since you have never been this way before.
Joshua 3:4 NIV

Soon, it will be football season again. During this time of year, I almost feel guilty not watching my husband's favorite teams play football pre-season, during season, and post-season. Not guilty enough to turn the TV on though! I grew up with a father and four brothers who watched or listened on the radio to every game that a certain team from Texas played. And we lived a few years in the DC area where the local team was next to godliness in many eyes! Here I have four boys and I can't get excited enough to turn the games on in order to pass on the generational love for the pigskin. Honestly, I don't think the boys care enough without a man to watch with.

But in the spirit of the game, I heard the phrase "game changer" recently in regard to my life and walk with Christ. I believe I have had several times in the recent past where I was on a path I had never been before, like the verse says, and only survived by keeping my spiritual eyes on God.

"Then"

When? Then I will know which way to go. At the point when you are at life's dead end, God carries you to the new road you are to take.

One "game changer" came when my husband lost his job. We were **not** in a place that would have made Dave Ramsey (the Christian financial advisor) proud! After a few months, I ventured out to find a job. I had been spending fifteen years raising my half dozen kids and not keeping up with my resume. The first interview I went to was for a position I figured out very quickly was not for me. I started to cry and wanted to apologize to the nice people for taking up their valuable time. I left feeling like I had no idea where God was going to lead me. I felt I had nothing to contribute to society. I sat sobbing in my car before driving home.

But for some reason I walked into a local Christian bookstore the next week believing that God was telling me which way to go. I was much more confident when I interviewed this time, even though nothing had changed except my belief that God was leading me there. And I got the job.

I fought God so hard, even though I KNEW He had provided this job for us. I hadn't gone "that way" before, like the verse. I hadn't worked outside the home. And here I was working for minimum wage and no benefits with a college education. But what better place? We started the day with prayer. Christian music played all day long. I worked with the most encouraging people. It was just the "way to go" for that stage in my life. A little cocoon, of sorts, that God kept me in. And I learned over time that it wasn't even about the money with God this time. He just needed to change some things in my heart.

The next "game changer" came when my husband passed away over Christmas break. Definitely a new direction I had never been before. Do I go back to work? Do I take time off? "Lord," I said, "I do not know what to do!" But like before, God carefully led me where He wanted me to be.

After a month off, I returned to work at the bookstore since my kids were in school and the youngest was still in our church's preschool program several days a week. What a blessing to return to that environment of the cocoon. The Christian music and the prayer time and the encouraging workers were just what I needed as I dealt with all the changes in my life. But that was only for a short season. It served its purpose and then God led me away. I needed to be more involved with my graduating senior. I needed to be home during this first summer without Dad. I was just needed at home for now. So that is the path I am on for now. God continues to keep me going, ready for the next "game changer".

What are some "game changers" that you have experienced recently in your life? We all can relate to the widow game changer but are there other ones that you have had to deal with within that new status? I encourage you, when you don't know which way to go, to look up. Look to Christ and the Scriptures to see where you are to go. It isn't often an easy "game changer". Most of the time, at least in my experience, it is painful. You know those plays in football where the guy catches the ball and gets hit mid-air from the opposite direction? That's what "game changers' feel like sometimes. They knock the breath right out of you. Didn't you feel like that when you became a widow? We are on a way we have never been before. A "game changer". So how are you going to handle it? Some days God and I are doing this widow thing "like a boss", as the young folks say. I am getting my family ready for school and church and we occasionally make it places on time. We are doing it. We are keeping going. Because Life Goes On. And God continues to lead us.

Let's thank God today for the "game changers" in our lives that draw us closer to Him and push us to be stronger than we ever thought possible.

Father God, It is hard to be thankful for the game changers in my life because they hurt and push me in ways I don't want to go so often. Thank You that as I am going a way I haven't been before, You are guiding me. Give me quiet moments to reflect on Your care during me new directions. And help me to see Your guiding hand in my life today. Amen

August 23
The Last Page?
By Linda Lint

All the days ordained for me were written in your book before one of them came to be.
Psalms 139:16 NIV

There it was, the last page. I knew that page was coming, and I dreaded it. I did not want to let go of this trusted journal. It was a gift from my beloved and held so many treasures. There were entries recording happy times of family holidays and birthdays. There were tear-stained pages as well, recording my beloved's illness and passing. Now it sat before me, open to the last blank page, waiting for words.

This is what I wrote:

The last words here in this journal he gave me. Tomorrow, the second anniversary of his home going, I will start another. I will treasure this one, because he gave it to me. It holds so much of my past. Yet, there is a new one waiting. It has blank pages, standing ready to take words – words that will document my life – all of the next chapters to come. For it is indeed true, God, You have a plan. All my days are recorded in Your book. There will be tear-stained pages in the new journal as well. However, there will also be tales of joy and Your provision and care. It will continue to be a record of my life serving You my God, Whom I love above all.

I do not believe it was a coincidence that this last entry was to happen on the eve of the two year anniversary. Since God Himself has written my book, I believe He planned it that way – because He wanted me to understand the truth of Psalm 139:16.

My beloved's book was completed in the early morning hours of a day two years ago. When he breathed his last, and the cover was closed, Jesus stood ready to usher him into his eternal home. My husband's earthly story is completed and now his eternal one is in place.

My book is not done. I have not yet reached the last page. There is more life for me to live – a life standing ready – waiting for the pages to be filled. Yes, it will be a different life – one I am to live without my beloved by my side. I know there will be tears and loneliness. I am still searching for direction and purpose. But, I do k.n.o.w. this - my life's story is authored by God Himself – written by His own hand before I was even formed in my mother's womb. *And I ask this – Isn't a life's story written by God's hand worth living?*

As I look ahead to the uncertain future, I say "yes" – yes to You God – this life is worth living. There are promises You have given me in another book – Your Word. You promise me in Jeremiah 29:11 that You have a plan and a purpose for hope; and in Psalm 138:8 that You will fulfill Your purpose for me.

Dear sisters, there is life left for you to live as well. Will you trust Him this day? I pray you will. Give Him all the as yet un-filled pages and watch what He does – marvel at the words He will inscribe on those pages. And when we each reach our own last pages, let us hear Him say – "That was a good story – now look at what I have written for you in eternity with Me!"

August 24
No Greater Love
By Rene Zonner

> *Greater love has no one than this:*
> *to lay down one's life for one's friends.*
> *John 15:13 NIV*

Would I be as far along in my grief journey without my friends?

I believe the answer is a resounding "No".

The three-year anniversary of my husband's death was this past summer and I found myself reflecting on how I've gotten to the healthy place I am today. Obviously, my faith in Jesus Christ has been the foundation of my healing. Even if I had nothing else or no one else, I would have Him. However, my Christian friends have played a large role in the healing my kids and I have experienced.

During those impossibly difficult first days, they stepped up in ways I would have never expected. The night John died, I had five dear friends drop everything to come and just be with me and be ready to do whatever was needed. One was eight and a half months pregnant at the time, and another drove more than two hours from a family vacation just to hug me and be there for a bit before driving back to her family the same night. Many, many friends came to the viewing and funeral to support me. Meals and childcare were provided. My oldest son's ninth birthday was just two days after the funeral and I asked for help with making a cake for his party. What I got was a full-blown party with decorations, food and gift bags. I can't even express to you how much that meant to us.

As much as the help and love in those first few months was helpful and precious, it has been the time invested in my family over the past few years that has been the most priceless.

I have had a handful of friends who have been in the trenches with me since day one of this new life of mine. Friends who have absorbed the kids and me into their families. Dear people who have listened and advised and cried with me as I have dealt with all the challenges widowhood brings. Christian brothers and sisters who have sacrificed family and personal time, offered financial gifts, and used their skills and experience to help me. Friends who have been walking right along beside me, cheering me on as I have learned to find my way in this new life. It's in each of these friends that I see Christ. It's through their hands that God has hugged me. It's in their words that the Holy Spirit has spoken words of comfort and peace to my heart. And it hasn't just been the friends I had before becoming a widow. Many of those I am closest to now are people I would have probably not met if it weren't for my situation. These friends have brought a new perspective to my life that older friends can't. Put the old and the new together and I have a community of love and support that I could never do without.

As much as I have been shown love through Christian friendship, I hope to show love back. See, there is a time when we need to take. When we are still healing and so deep in the grief, we need others to pour into us. But eventually, we move through the toughest parts of grief and when we do it's time to give. I believe God gives us friends and family to support us and help grow us in our widowhood. At some point, though, He expects us to mature and be ready to support others. It may mean that you mentor another widow who is not as far along in her journey, maybe you take a divorced, single mom under your wing, or you just step up in a time of need for one of those who was there for you in the darkest days.

Is it your turn to give your life for a friend? Is it time to step up and walk the walk with another? Who can you show Christ's love to as it was shown to you?

Father, I am so grateful for Christ-like friends who show Your love to me on a regular basis. Help me, Lord, to know when it's time to give to others the same friendship and love I have received. Open my heart and mind to see those for whom I can lay down my life as others have laid down theirs for me. Amen

August 25
His Blessings Will Come
By Sheryl Pepple

Blessed are you who hunger now, for you will be satisfied.
Blessed are you who weep now, for you will laugh.
Luke 6:21 NIV

I remember early in my journey as a new widow I wondered if I would ever truly laugh again. Not just a polite sound that mimicked a laugh when appropriate for the conversation, but a deep healthy laugh. A carefree laugh. A laugh like I used to laugh before my husband died...

For the last week I have been extremely blessed by the visit of a long-time friend (notice I carefully did not say old friend). It is so interesting to see how God has used her visit as a time for healing in so many ways.

We were friends for many, many years and we went on vacations together with our spouses. Somehow life got busy and we both ended up moving to different states. Even in this wonderful age of technology, we ended up not keeping in touch with each other. By the time my husband Dave passed away, I wasn't even sure how to get a hold of her. One day, out of the blue, I got an email from her (she found me on Facebook) and we reconnected. Then about six months ago her son started going to a school near me, and she started visiting me periodically. Our friendship has resumed as if we never missed a beat even though there was a six-year gap, and many significant life changing events that occurred in both our lives during that time.

It has been such a treasure to rekindle with a friend who knew and loved my husband. We get to share our memories. She knew him so well that she knows what he would be thinking and feeling if he were physically here during this phase of my life. What a joy it has been to be able to share that with someone. But God has brought her back into my life to bless me in another way. He has delivered on His promise that those who weep now - will laugh.

It is hard to really describe my friend, but I guess I would say that laughter is just such a part of who she is at her very core. Even when she is going through difficult times, laughter is a mainstay on her so-called diet. She has a gift for finding ways to laugh in almost any situation. Her three-day visit has extended into a ten-day visit (I think she prefers the Texas weather over the weather in Wisconsin) and I find myself healing and laughing all along the way. God is so faithful and He will fulfill His promises.

Dear sisters, you may be so new on your journey that this seems impossible. If that is where you are, that is okay. I pray that God will just tuck this promise into your heart for encouragement for the future. Some of you may be at the stage where you have started to laugh but it feels strange, maybe even fake. I found that to be a difficult stage, because it increased my fear that I would never be okay again. As I have continued to walk this journey, God is delivering me into a new season, a season of healing, where the laughter feels real again. He has delivered on His promise!

Dear Heavenly Father, thank You so much for being who You are - a God who is faithful. I thank You that Your Word tells me that You are always with me and that You never leave me. I thank You also that Your Word tells me that those who weep now, will laugh again. Your mercies are new each day and I am grateful for all of Your provisions, for all my needs. In Your Son's Holy and Precious Name, Amen

August 26
Lost
By Rene Zonner

Even though I walk through the valley of the shadow of death;
I will fear no evil:
for you are with me;

Psalm 23:4 NIV

I lost an earring.

A special earring.

This earring was one from the pair my husband had given me on what turned out to be our last Christmas together.

I loved those earrings.

Even before John's death, these earrings were special. It was one of the few times my husband bought me jewelry. They weren't fancy or expensive but they were exactly my style. It was obvious that he had put thought and effort into picking them out and it meant so much. After he died, they became even more precious since they were a visible reminder of John's love. I was able to wear the earrings even when I felt it was time to take off my wedding rings. I wore them every day and it felt like I had a little piece of John with me each time I did.

I actually lost one of these earrings before. Just a few months after John died, I looked in the mirror and realized I only had one earring. I panicked. I started crying and almost hyper-ventilated. My poor children were very freaked out. I felt like a terrible person for being so careless. How could I lose something so precious? Losing that earring brought much of my grief right up to the surface and it hurt. Then a miracle happened. A few hours after I realized the earring was lost, my youngest son found it just lying on the kitchen floor. I had looked everywhere for that earring! I was confused how he had managed to find it somewhere I had searched but, more than anything, I was happy it was found. My grief was still so fresh and I needed that physical connection the earrings gave me.

Over the last few years I continued to wear the earrings but, had lost the need and desire to wear them every day. I'd wear them when I was particularly missing John, or when I was lonely and needed a reminder I was once loved, or when I just wanted to feel a connection with him again. Some people visit the grave of their husband…I wore the earrings.

Now I've lost one of them again. And I'm pretty sure it's gone for good this time. No second miracle. But you know what? It's okay. Oh, I am sad to have lost it and I miss wearing them. I'm disappointed I won't be able to pass them on to my daughter someday. But I don't feel the deep sense of loss that I did the first time it was lost.

That's when I realized I had truly made it to the other side of the dark valley of grief.

I will always miss John and, if I had my way, he would still be here with me and the kids. This journey has been long and the hardest thing I have ever done. But, I've walked it with God at my side, leading me and carrying me. Psalm 23:4 says "Even though I walk *through* the valley of the shadow of death, I will fear no evil: for you are with me;" Did you catch it? We walk THROUGH the valley of death. We don't stay there. The heavy burden of grief does end. God comforts us while we are in it and He gently leads us to the other side.

Friends, I know many of you are still in the valley and are hurting deeply. Please hear me when I tell you it won't always be this dark. Cling to God and allow him to lead you through the valley. I promise you the view on the other side is amazing!

Father, I ask that I will be able to feel Your presence. Walk with me, carry me, and lead me to the other side Lord. I praise You that I don't have to stay in the valley and thank You in advance for the time to come when I am out of the darkness. Amen

August 27
A Recovering Worrier....
by Nancy Howell

Don't fret or worry. Instead of worrying, pray. Let petitions and praises shape your worries into prayers, letting God know your concerns. Before you know it, a sense of God's wholeness, everything coming together for good, will come and settle you down. It's wonderful what happens when Christ displaces worry at the center of your life.

Philippians 4:6-7 The Message

Hmmm....read that again, sisters. That passage, so beautifully translated by The Message, gives very simple directions. *"Don't fret or worry..."*

Hello. My name is Nancy. I am a worrier.

Let me rephrase that—I am a recovering worrier. Much like other addicting habits of indulgence, worrying is hard to wrestle free from.

I should know, I've struggled with the addiction of worry the majority of my life. Worry nags at you, whispering quietly, "You're not good enough..." "you'll never finish this project on time" "you're unprepared, per usual!"

My spouse was not a worrier. In fact, he remains the most laid-back, easy going, put together person I have ever known. Whenever he would sense (or hear) my angst, he had one response: "Sweetie, worrying doesn't do you any good. Nothing productive comes from worry. Do your best, let it go, and always remember 'EGBAR'....Everything's Going to Be Alright!" And with that, he'd go on his merry way.

Sometimes I swear I could hear him whistling a happy tune as our conversation concluded. Throughout our years together, during particular situations he simply would look into my eyes, smile and say, "EGBAR." He knew I needed reminding. And it helped.

After his death, I didn't worry about anything. Call me crazy (and you wouldn't be the first!), but for months I was on auto-pilot.

Looking back, I realize I didn't worry because I was bathed in God's light. I felt as if my boys and I were being carried around on the most comfortable mattresses possible, with nothing around nearby to touch or harm us. We were completely surrounded by prayers, protected from the world.

Unfortunately, that total feeling of comfort and protection did not last. I began to relapse back into old habits, worrying about our sons, finances, major life decisions, future goals, life in general. I no longer had Mark alongside me, whispering "EGBAR".

I struggled to leave the worrying at God's feet, praying for answers to questions nagging at my soul. As I cleaned up my kitchen late one night, I glanced at the plaque prominently displayed by my sink. Given to me by Mark's special angel, his ICU nurse who lovingly cared for him during his last days here on earth, it quotes Philippians 4:13.

God makes it so simple. Why do we have to make it so hard?

"Instead of worrying, pray…"

Give your petitions and worries to God, fashioning them into prayers. Your concerns matter to Him.

"Before you know it, a sense of God's wholeness, everything coming together for good, will come and settle you down…"

August 28
A Recovering Worrier... Continued
by Nancy Howell

I've often read that the absence of fear is faith. Faith is believing that God will bring you through whatever situation you are in.

As widows, we come to God's throne in many different circumstances. Some of us struggle with loneliness, while others may be financially strapped.

Some have to uproot and move to strange new surroundings, soon after losing our significant others. Others are left alone with child rearing responsibilities. And believe me, it takes both a mother and a father when possible to raise a child in the way that God wants.

Whatever our personal situation, our spiritual circumstances can be the same. Have faith, not fear. Allow your Heavenly Father to tote your heavy load. His shoulders are strong and He can handle whatever you put at His feet. *"everything coming together for good, will come and settle you down..."*

If the absence of fear is faith, I want to proclaim that the absence of worry is trust.

The absence of worry is TRUST. As my sweet husband told me countless times, worry doesn't do anyone any good—except the devil. He is behind your worries. He is the one whispering you aren't capable. He is the one causing you to lose sleep as a dozen different issues run through your mind. Don't give him the satisfaction. There's only One that can silence him—God.

God is beside you. Regardless. He is simply waiting for you to TRUST Him to take your worries.

Remember, there's nothing that our God cannot do. Surrendering, trusting, giving your burdens to Him, even in the midst of enormous grief and shifting sand, can free you. Free you to be what God wants you to be.

He has a plan. It may not be the plan you wanted, but it's a plan, nonetheless. Leave your worries at His feet.

"It's wonderful what happens when Christ displaces worry at the center of your life.."

In worry's place? Trust. Pure, loving, simple, and soothing.

EGBAR, dear sisters. If God, Jesus, and the Holy Spirit are for us, who can be against us?

Dear Father, I praise Your name for the ability to take all of my worries. Help me let go of them. It's hard to let go, walk away, and not try to pick them back up. That's where trust comes in. We trust You to handle the worrying part. Transform me so that worry is no longer the center of our existence. I want You to be the center. Thank You most of all for Your patience as I give You my all. In Jesus' name I ask it all, Amen.

August 29
Music Heals!
By Teri Cox

> *The LORD your God is in your midst,*
> *a mighty one who will save;*
> *he will rejoice over you with gladness;*
> *he will quiet you by his love;*
> *he will exult over you with loud singing.*
> Zephaniah 3:16 ESV

There is a place deep within where music meets my soul and spirit in unison. It is at a depth like nothing else in my world. Neither spoken nor written word can reach that place; video production and live scenes offer connection but not at the depth that music reaches me. Since losing my beloved, almost two years ago, music has been a constant source of healing. It has brought tears and memories, laugher and familiarity.

Daryl and I met through music at our church. He was the drummer and I was a vocalist on the worship team. God brought us together through songs that sang His praises and it was ALWAYS part of our life journey. Daryl's Celebration of Life had a mini praise and worship service. It was the only way he could be sent Home; through music. It was an incredible part of his life and had to be part of our final farewell for him.

As I sat to write tonight, there was a lovely old hymn that caught my ear: "Jesus, Jesus, how I trust Him! How I've proved Him o'er and o'er Jesus, Jesus, precious Jesus! O for grace to trust Him more!" What beautiful and yet difficult words. This hymn, 'Tis So Sweet To Trust In Jesus, was written in 1882 by Louisa M. R. Stead. She, her daughter and her husband went on a picnic, one summer afternoon, on Long Island Sound. They heard a cry for help and Mr. Stead jumped into the water. As Louisa and her daughter Lily stood on the bank and watched, Mr. Stead and the boy he jumped in to save both drowned.

Louisa M. R. Stead became a widow on a warm summer day. It certainly was not part of her plan. She had no warning, no way of knowing when she packed that picnic basket. Her life became infinitely more difficult due to poverty and trials. Yet, out of the deep waters came service and song. Louisa and Lily became South African missionaries and this beautiful hymn became Louisa's cry of trust.

Trust is a choice, sisters; not an easy one or an automatic one, but one that can be found through grace. Remembering that grace is not anything about us but everything about God; it's His unmerited favor. We do not earn it. We do not deserve it. We simply receive it. I pray you trust and peace today. God has already gone before you and He **will** carry you through. He rejoices over you and He sings over you. You will find your heart song again.

August 30
Lady in Waiting
By Julie Wright

I wait for the Lord, my whole being waits,
and in his word I put my hope.
I wait for the Lord more than watchmen wait for the morning
Psalm 130:5-6 NIV

Blessed are all who wait for him.
Isaiah 30:18b NIV

I have co-workers and friends who are always asking me about different things going on in my life.

What's going on with the foreclosure? Any word yet? "I'm still waiting to hear from the courts."

How's the house hunting going? "I'm still waiting for the right one."

How's the insurance claim going? "I'm still waiting on the adjustor to call me back."

How are the kids feeling? "I'm still waiting for the antibiotics to kick in."

How are you celebrating Thanksgiving this year? "I'm still waiting to hear if my parents will make it down or not."

Any word on your sister-in-law's surgery yet? "We're still waiting to hear from the doctors."

It seems like I'm constantly waiting for things to start happening or for the right timing of other situations. We joke about it all the time at work. My dear and trusted friends have dubbed me the "Lady-in-Waiting."

Most of us don't like waiting though. We don't like waiting in the long lines at the grocery store. We don't like waiting in traffic. We don't like waiting at the doctor's office. We don't like waiting for test results. We don't like waiting to hear if someone has safely arrived. We don't like waiting when a child is arriving home way past their curfew.

Waiting just plain stinks.

As a widow, it stinks even more. I really hate waiting for a table at a restaurant by myself. (If I'm even brave enough to venture out on my own to begin with).

I hate waiting in the pew at church, wondering if anyone will stop and say "hello" or offer to sit next to me.

I hate waiting to hear from the doctor, especially with no one here to help calm my wandering fears and anxiety.

I hate waiting and wondering if God will send someone into my life to share the next 40-50 years with me.

I looked up the word waiting in the dictionary, just out of curiosity. Waiting is defined as to stay, to linger, to tarry, or abide.

It seems to me that I do those things a lot. I tend to linger, to tarry in the past. Wishing my husband was here to hold my hand. Waiting for him to come through the door and give me my daily bear hug and kiss. Lingering in the walk-in closet, caressing his leather jacket as if it will make him appear before me.

The last part of the definition really hit me though. To abide. That has a completely different appeal to me. To abide; it means to dwell with, to reside near, to stay. That's what God wants me to do in these long, lonely days of widowhood. He hastens me to come and dwell with him…tuck in under His wings and just rest. Snuggle in tightly and closely so the only sound I hear is the rhythm of his breath and heartbeat.

Waiting. Although at times it's not fun or pleasant, it has much peace and power. I've learned three things that we can do while we are "ladies-in-waiting."

First, love God. *"Love the Lord your God with all your heart, with all your soul and with all your strength." Deut. 6:1*

No matter what we are waiting for, we can always love God. The sad part is that God is always waiting for us to love him back. We're the ones who continue to linger and tarry, dragging our feet through the past or trying to carve out a path in the future before its even time, instead of residing in His promises. He's always ready and waiting for us to love him. That's a simple request that we can easily fulfill while we wait.

Second, serve others. *"Serve one another in love."* *Gal. 5:13*

So much time is wasted while we are waiting and worrying about things or situations that are either out of our control or cannot be changed. Instead of impatiently stomping our feet while we wait, why not help someone else out while we can. Serving others will certainly take your mind off of the things that we are waiting for and sometimes serving others makes us realize that what we were waiting for, we didn't truly need to begin with.

Third, tell others about Him. *"Proclaim (announce) the power of God."* *Psalm 68:34*

We tend to put ourselves in a "waiting" bubble and forget to share our worries or concerns with others who would eagerly join us in prayer, service or praise, if we would only let them in. Share with friends and strangers the feelings or anxieties you may be having about the upcoming holiday time. I'd venture to say that most people would love to offer a shoulder to cry on, a warm cup of coffee to sip, or a meal to bring warmth to your belly and soul, if we would only let them know our needs. When those friends reach out to you, share how God has comforted you, provided for you, or even sometimes felt far away. I'm almost certain that most could relate to all of those feelings at one time or another.

So, if you are a "lady-in-waiting", I hope that you will choose to wait in his care. He promises us that we are loved and that we have a purpose created just for us by him. Let's not waste any more time waiting, but more time abiding in God and His Word. I hope you'll take time this week to join me at the bottom of the cross. I'll be the one abiding there with arms wide open. Thanks for "waiting" there with me.

August 31
Wiggling Towards the Stirring Waters
By Kit Hinkle

"Sir," the invalid replied, "I have no one to help me into the pool when the water is stirred. While I am trying to get in, someone else goes down ahead of me."

John 5:7 NIV

I had Joyce Meyers speak at my church today. What an amazing light she is.

She spoke about something widows need to hear. That is, about moving forward. Over and over she brought out examples from her life and examples from the Bible where Christ commands us to move forward.

Here was the first example: When Moses died, the Israelites mourned for thirty days, and then, as Jewish law required, they ended their mourning. Of course it takes longer than thirty days to move past grief, but still, God spoke up and even said, "Moses my servant is dead. Now then, you and all these people, get ready to cross the Jordan River into the land I am about to give to them--to the Israelites." (Joshua 1:2).

God knows we need to grieve. He also knows He has a plan for us. So, once the initial grief has passed, to spend most of our energies focusing primarily on grief when He wants so much more for us may hold us back from the blessings he has in store.

Joyce Meyers gave an example from her own life, explaining the abuse both she and her brother endured as children, and the difficulty she went through accepting it and then letting go of the victim role so that God could use her mightily. Her brother wasn't as able to. He spun out of control, and she came to his rescue over and over, until finally she let him go on his own. He fell apart again and eventually died from consequences of his behavior. The two siblings' stories had stark differences. Both started as victims. Both were given unlimited opportunity—one stayed a victim and died. One grabbed hold of Christ and let Him use her for His kingdom.

Do you believe God will use you? Can you reach out and let Him move you forward so that your life from here out will be great?

One more example she used—remember John Chapter five when Jesus meets the cripple by the stirring waters of the pool where the sick are healed? The cripple complained to Jesus that he and been there thirty-eight years and can't seem to get to the water before anyone else does, so he can't get healed. Joyce Meyers told us—"watch this". She went to the edge of the stage and lay down. "Okay," she said. "Pretend I can't walk." She wiggled her shoulders and arms, but kept her legs immobile. She wiggled and wiggled and almost wiggled herself off the edge of the stage. Then she got up. "You think after thirty-eight years, eventually I'd perch myself so close to the edge of the water, that when that angel came to stir it up, I'd be the first one to go plop—right in the drink."

What's holding you back from the edge of your pool? Can you get in? Can you stop letting the hurt from your past keep you on the sidelines?

Dear Lord, Encourage me today. Open up my world to new purpose and hope. Show me how many lives can be changed if just this one widow steps up and moves forward through my pain into new life with You. Amen.

Topical Index:

Writer Index:

Connect With Us:

We hope you enjoyed these daily devotions. We have more ways to connect with A Widow's Might/aNew Season Ministries.

- Social Media: twitter (@anewseas @AWidowsMight); facebook (aNew Season Ministries, A Widow's Might)
- Website **www.anewseason.net**
- Conference (November, 2014 Myrtle Beach)
- Retreats (Ruth Training Retreats)
- Blogs
- Be a Guest Blogger (request info on our website)
- Prayer requests can be submitted on our facebook page or our website
- Coming soon – the next season of daily devotions! Look for the Fall Edition in the fall of 2014!

Made in the USA
Lexington, KY
01 June 2014